POE

WILLIA

POEMS OF WILLIAM BLAKE

Selected and Introduced by

Peter Ackroyd

SINCLAIR-STEVENSON

First published in Great Britain in 1995
by Sinclair-Stevenson
an imprint of Reed Consumer Books Ltd
Michelin House, 81 Fulham Road, London SW3 6RB
and Auckland, Melbourne, Singapore and Toronto

A CIP catalogue record for this book
is available at the British Library
ISBN 1 85619 562 7

Typeset by Deltatype Ltd, Ellesmere Port, Cheshire
Printed and bound in Great Britain
by Cox & Wyman Ltd, Reading, Berkshire

Contents

Introduction

William Blake wrote poems which are as familiar as any in the English language; there can be few people who have not at some time sung 'Jerusalem' or chanted 'The Tyger'. It is something of a paradox, then, that most of Blake's other verse remains unread. For a hundred readers of his most famous collection, *Songs of Innocence and of Experience*, there is perhaps one who has ventured into the distant realms of his prophetic books. Epics such as *Milton* and *Jerusalem* are quite neglected, while only a few scholars and academics have studied such wonderful poems as *The Four Zoas* and *The Book of Urizen*. Yet it is here that Blake's true achievement, and evidence of his real genius, are to be found. If he had never written anything other than these long poems, he would still be the greatest English poet of his age.

Of course they are generally considered to be complex, obscure and for all practical purposes unreadable – the effusions, in short, of a disordered or excessively idiosyncratic imagination. T. S. Eliot set that critical trend when he accused Blake of being an ill-educated autodidact who was denied the benefits of a 'tradition' in which to place himself. All that was nonsense, but even Blake's admirers – from Swinburne and Rossetti to Chesterton and Lindsay – have felt it necessary to excuse rather than applaud his prophetic books. It is my intention, in this short selection, to redress that balance. It is my belief, in fact, that much of Blake's epic poetry is as lucid and as comprehensible as anything to be found within his shorter lyrics. There are certain difficulties of terminology, but these are not insurmountable; Blake was trying single-handedly to create a vocabulary which would express his visionary comprehension of his own time, so there is some reason to forgive his occasional longueurs. His denunciation of mechanical science will probably find a more sympathetic audience now than it has done for the last two hundred years; and his association of war with thwarted phallic sexuality anticipates the work of Freud in the early twentieth century. These are indeed two of his central themes; once their purport is understood, his neologisms and allusions fall into place. There is also the question of the myth which he invented, complete with a cast of visionary characters and places; but it is not necessary to follow every twist or embellishment of the plot in order to recognise that he is setting out his own history of Creation and Fall. His saga is that of humanity fallen from its divine state, divided into various warring faculties, perceptions attenuated and vision dimmed. Once this principal element is grasped, the real work of understanding has been achieved. In this selection, too, I have tried to include passages which are self-contained or at least self-explanatory. One significant element of his poetic work cannot be included, however; his poetry was always illustrated or, rather, his poems were part of an integrated pictorial design. I would urge anyone who is remotely interested in the texts which follow to find and consult facsimile reproductions of what are, after all, 'illuminated' works.

It would be true to say, of course, that Blake's life work was a failure in his own time. He created a public voice, close to the popular ballads and dramas of the period, but he never found a public. Only a few enthusiasts cared about his art – and fewer still knew anything about his poetry. He once said that it would take two hundred years for the artistic genius of his friend Henry Fuseli to be recognised; the same precept might equally well be applied to him, which is perhaps why this selection of his verse comes at an opportune moment. I have chosen many of the shorter lyrics by which he is still principally known; no one can ignore such masterpieces of dramatic irony as 'The Sick Rose' or 'London'. I also felt it worth including poems from his first production, *Poetical Sketches*, if only to demonstrate how pure and subtle an ear he possessed even in early youth. I have then embarked upon the less familiar aspects of his work, beginning with the complete version of *The Book of Thel*. This is a wonderful pastoral lament which requires no especial knowledge or information to understand. Similarly, from *The Marriage of Heaven and Hell* I have selected the 'Proverbs of Hell', which display Blake's aphoristic gifts at their most powerful and intense. From the later epics, both short and long, I have taken those passages that exemplify the grand simplicity of his essential vision. In *Visions of the Daughters of Albion*, for example, Blake is concerned with the restriction of sexual expression, and the attendant growth of sexual jealousy, as part of the general diminution of human perception. *America* and *The French Revolution* address contemporary events within the context of heroic and biblical narrative. *Europe, The Song of Los* and *The Book of Urizen* are concerned with what might now be termed the psychology of repression as well as the whole history of religious and cultural restraint. I have taken from two of his longer epics, *Milton* and *Jerusalem*, those passages which demonstrate the clarity of his polemic or the beauty of his lyric gift. I have also included lines from *Vala* or *The Four Zoas*, a long poem which remained unknown and unpublished until the end of the nineteenth century; here, almost hidden from view, is some of the finest poetry in the language. That is why it is time, I believe, for Blake's true value to be appreciated beyond the bounds of the university or scholarly monograph.

Peter Ackroyd
London, 1995

NOTE ON THE TEXT

I have decided to retain the original spelling and punctuation, both of Blake's lyrics and prophecies, simply because they are an integral part of his work. Otherwise, too, there would be no end to editorial revision.

From *Poetical Sketches*

To Spring

O thou, with dewy locks, who lookest down
Thro' the clear windows of the morning; turn
Thine angel eyes upon our western isle,
Which in full choir hails thy approach, O Spring!

The hills tell each other, and the list'ning
Vallies hear; all our longing eyes are turned
Up to thy bright pavillions: issue forth,
And let thy holy feet visit our clime.

Come o'er the eastern hills, and let our winds
Kiss thy perfumed garments; let us taste
Thy morn and evening breath; scatter thy pearls
Upon our love-sick land that mourns for thee.

O deck her forth with thy fair fingers; pour
Thy soft kisses on her bosom; and put
Thy golden crown upon her languish'd head,
Whose modest tresses were bound up for thee!

To the Evening Star

Thou fair-hair'd angel of the evening,
Now, whilst the sun rests on the mountains, light
Thy bright torch of love; thy radiant crown
Put on, and smile upon our evening bed!
Smile on our loves; and, while thou drawest the
Blue curtains of the sky, scatter thy silver dew
On every flower that shuts its sweet eyes
In timely sleep. Let thy west wind sleep on
The lake; speak silence with thy glimmering eyes,
And wash the dusk with silver. Soon, full soon,
Dost thou withdraw; then the wolf rages wide,
And the lion glares thro' the dun forest:
The fleeces of our flocks are cover'd with
Thy sacred dew: protect them with thine influence.

Song

How sweet I roam'd from field to field,
  And tasted all the summer's pride,
'Till I the prince of love beheld,
  Who in the sunny beams did glide!

He shew'd me lilies for my hair,
  And blushing roses for my brow;
He led me through his gardens fair,
  Where all his golden pleasures grow.

With sweet May dews my wings were wet,
  And Phoebus fir'd my vocal rage;
He caught me in his silken net,
  And shut me in his golden cage.

He loves to sit and hear me sing,
  Then, laughing, sports and plays with me;
Then stretches out my golden wing,
  And mocks my loss of liberty.

The conclusion of *Tiriel*

He said. O weak mistaken father of a lawless race
Thy laws O Har & Tiriels wisdom end together in a curse
Why is one law given to the lion & the patient Ox
And why men bound beneath the heavens in a reptile form
A worm of sixty winters creeping on the dusky ground
The child springs from the womb. the father ready stands to form
The infant head while the mother idle plays with her dog on her couch
The young bosom is cold for lack of mothers nourishment & milk
Is cut off from the weeping mouth with difficulty & pain
The little lids are lifted & the little nostrils opend
The father forms a whip to rouze the sluggish senses to act
And scourges off all youthful fancies from the newborn man
Then walks the weak infant in sorrow compelld to number footsteps
Upon the sand.
And when the drone has reachd his crawling length
Black berries appear that poison all around him. Such was Tiriel
Compelld to pray repugnant & to humble the immortal spirit
Till I am subtil as a serpent in a paradise
Consuming all both flowers & fruits insects & warbling birds
And now my paradise is falln & a drear sandy plain
Returns my thirsty hissings in a curse on thee O Har
Mistaken father of a lawless race my voice is past
He ceast outstretchd at Har & Hevas feet in awful death.

The Book of Thel

Thel's Motto

Does the Eagle know what is in the pit?
Or wilt thou go ask the Mole:
Can Wisdom be put in a silver rod?
Or Love in a golden bowl?

I

The daughters of Mne Seraphim led round their sunny flocks.
All but the youngest; she in paleness sought the secret air.
To fade away like morning beauty from her mortal day:
Down by the river of Adona her soft voice is heard:
And thus her gentle lamentation falls like morning dew.

O life of this our spring! why fades the lotus of the water?
Why fade these children of the spring? born but to smile & fall.
Ah! Thel is like a watry bow. and like a parting cloud.
Like a reflection in a glass. like shadows in the water.
Like dreams of infants. like a smile upon an infants face,
Like the doves voice, like transient day, like music in the air;
Ah! gentle may I lay me down, and gentle rest my head.
And gentle sleep the sleep of death. and gentle hear the voice
Of him that walketh in the garden in the evening time.

The Lilly of the valley breathing in the humble grass
Answer'd the lovely maid and said; I am a watry weed,
And I am very small, and love to dwell in lowly vales;
So weak, the gilded butterfly scarce perches on my head.
Yet I am visited from heaven and he that smiles on all.
Walks in the valley. and each morn over me spreads his hand
Saying, rejoice thou humble grass, thou new-born lilly flower,
Thou gentle maid of silent valleys. and of modest brooks;
For thou shalt be clothed in light, and fed with morning manna:
Till summers heat melts thee beside the fountains and the springs
To flourish in eternal vales: then why should Thel complain,
Why should the mistress of the vales of Har, utter a sigh.
She ceasd & smild in tears, then sat down in her silver shrine.

Thel answerd. O thou little virgin of the peaceful valley.
Giving to those that cannot crave, the voiceless, the o'erfired.
Thy breath doth nourish the innocent lamb, he smells thy milky
garments,
He crops thy flowers. while thou sittest smiling in his face,
Wiping his mild and meekin mouth from all contagious taints.
Thy wine doth purify the golden honey, thy perfume,
Which thou dost scatter on every little blade of grass that springs
Revives the milked cow, & tames the fire-breathing steed.
But Thel is like a faint cloud kindled at the rising sun:
I vanish from my pearly throne, and who shall find my place.

Queen of the vales the Lilly answerd, ask the tender cloud,
And it shall tell thee why it glitters in the morning sky,
And why it scatters its bright beauty thro' the humid air.
Descend O little cloud & hover before the eyes of Thel.
The Cloud descended, and the Lilly bowd her modest head:
And went to mind her numerous charge among the verdant grass.

II

O little Cloud the virgin said, I charge thee tell to me,
Why thou complainest not when in one hour thou fade away:
Then we shall seek thee but not find; ah Thel is like to thee.
I pass away. yet I complain, and no one hears my voice.

The Cloud then shew'd his golden head & his bright form emerg'd,
Hovering and glittering on the air before the face of Thel.
O virgin know'st thou not. our steeds drink of the golden springs
Where Luvah doth renew his horses: look'st thou on my youth,
And fearest thou because I vanish and am seen no more.
Nothing remains; O maid I tell thee, when I pass away,
It is to tenfold life, to love, to peace, and raptures holy:
Unseen descending, weigh my light wings upon balmy flowers;
And court the fair eyed dew. to take me to her shining tent;
The weeping virgin, trembling kneels before the risen sun,
Till we arise link'd in a golden band, and never part;
But walk united, bearing food to all our tender flowers

Dost thou O little Cloud? I fear that I am not like thee;
For I walk through the vales of Har. and smell the sweetest
flowers;
But I feed not the little flowers: I hear the warbling birds,
But I feed not the warbling birds. they fly and seek their food;

But Thel delights in these no more because I fade away,
And all shall say, without a use this shining woman liv'd,
Or did she only live. to be at death the food of worms.

The Cloud reclind upon his airy throne and answer'd thus.
Then if thou art the food of worms. O virgin of the skies,
How great thy use. how great thy blessing; every thing that lives,
Lives not alone, nor for itself: fear not and I will call
The weak worm from its lowly bed, and thou shalt hear its voice.
Come forth worm of the silent valley, to thy pensive queen.
The helpless worm arose, and sat upon the Lillys leaf,
And the bright Cloud saild on, to find his partner in the vale.

III

Then Thel astonish'd view'd the Worm upon its dewy bed.

Art thou a Worm? image of weakness. art thou but a Worm?
I see thee like an infant wrapped in the Lillys leaf:
Ah weep not little voice, thou can'st not speak. but thou can'st weep;
Is this a Worm? I see thee lay helpless & naked: weeping,
And none to answer, none to cherish thee with mothers smiles.

The Clod of Clay heard the Worms voice, & raisd her pitying head;
She bow'd over the weeping infant, and her life exhal'd
In milky fondness, then on Thel she fix'd her humble eyes.
O beauty of the vales of Har. we live not for ourselves,
Thou seest me the meanest thing, and so I am indeed;
My bosom of itself is cold. and of itself is dark,
But he that loves the lowly, pours his oil upon my head.
And kisses me, and binds his nuptial bands around my breast.
And says; Thou mother of my children, I have loved thee.
And I have given thee a crown that none can take away
But how this is sweet maid, I know not, and I cannot know,
I ponder, and I cannot ponder; yet I live and love.

The daughter of beauty wip'd her pitying tears with her white veil
And said. Alas! I knew not this, and therefore did I weep:
That God would love a Worm I knew, and punish the evil foot
That wilful, bruis'd its helpless form: but that he cherish'd it
With milk and oil, I never knew; and therefore did I weep,
And I complained in the mild air, because I fade away,
And lay me down in thy cold bed, and leave my shining lot.

Queen of the vales, the matron Clay answerd; I heard thy sighs.
And all thy moans flew o'er my roof. but I have call'd them down:
Wilt thou O Queen enter my house. 'tis given thee to enter,
And to return; fear nothing. enter with thy virgin feet.

IV

The eternal gates terrific porter lifted the northern bar:
Thel enter'd in & saw the secrets of the land unknown;
She saw the couches of the dead, & where the fibrous roots
Of every heart on earth infixes deep its restless twists:
A land of sorrows & of tears where never smile was seen.

She wanderd in the land of clouds thro' valleys dark, listning
Dolours & lamentations: waiting oft beside a dewy grave
She stood in silence. listning to the voices of the ground,
Till to her own grave plot she came, & there she sat down.
And heard this voice of sorrow breathed from the hollow pit.

Why cannot the Ear be closed to its own destruction?
Or the glistning Eye to the poison of a smile!
Why are Eyelids stord with arrows ready drawn,
Where a thousand fighting men in ambush lie?
Or an Eye of gifts & graces, show'ring fruits & coined gold!
Why a Tongue impress'd with honey from every wind?
Why an Ear, a whirlpool fierce to draw creations in?
Why a Nostril wide inhaling terror trembling & affright.
Why a tender curb upon the youthful burning boy!
Why a little curtain of flesh on the bed of our desire?

The Virgin started from her seat, & with a shriek.
Fled back unhinderd till she came into the vales of Har.

Poems from *Songs of Innocence*

Introduction

Piping down the valleys wild
Piping songs of pleasant glee
On a cloud I saw a child.
And he laughing said to me.

Pipe a song about a Lamb;
So I piped with merry chear,
Piper pipe that song again –
So I piped, he wept to hear.

Drop thy pipe thy happy pipe
Sing thy songs of happy chear,
So I sung the same again
While he wept with joy to hear

Piper sit thee down and write
In a book that all may read –
So he vanish'd from my sight.
And I pluck'd a hollow reed.

And I made a rural pen,
And I stain'd the water clear,
And I wrote my happy songs
Every child may joy to hear.

The Shepherd

How sweet is the Shepherds sweet lot,
From the morn to the evening he strays:
He shall follow his sheep all the day
And his tongue shall be filled with praise.

For he hears the lambs innocent call,
And he hears the ewes tender reply,
He is watchful while they are in peace,
For they know when their Shepherd is nigh.

The Ecchoing Green

The Sun does arise,
And make happy the skies.
The merry bells ring
To welcome the Spring.
The sky-lark and thrush,
The birds of the bush,
Sing louder around,
To the bells chearful sound.
While our sports shall be seen
On the Ecchoing Green.

Old John with white hair
Does laugh away care,
Sitting under the oak,
Among the old folk,
They laugh at our play,
And soon they all say.
Such such were the joys.
When we all girls & boys,
In our youth-time were seen,
On the Ecchoing Green.

Till the little ones weary
No more can be merry
The sun does descend,
And our sports have an end:
Round the laps of their mothers,
Many sisters and brothers,
Like birds in their nest,
Are ready for rest;
And sport no more seen,
On the darkening Green.

The Lamb

Little Lamb who made thee
Dost thou know who made thee
Gave thee life & bid thee feed.
By the stream & o'er the mead;
Gave thee clothing of delight,
Softest clothing wooly bright;
Gave thee such a tender voice,
Making all the vales rejoice!
Little Lamb who made thee
Dost thou know who made thee

Little Lamb I'll tell thee,
Little Lamb I'll tell thee!
He is called by thy name,
For he calls himself a Lamb:
He is meek & he is mild,
He became a little child:
I a child & thou a lamb,
We are called by his name,
Little Lamb God bless thee.
Little Lamb God bless thee.

The Little Black Boy

My mother bore me in the southern wild,
And I am black, but O! my soul is white;
White as an angel is the English child:
But I am black as if bereav'd of light.

My mother taught me underneath a tree
And sitting down before the heat of day,
She took me on her lap and kissed me,
And pointing to the east began to say.

Look on the rising sun: there God does live
And gives his light, and gives his heat away.
And flowers and trees and beasts and men recieve
Comfort in morning joy in the noon day.

And we are put on earth a little space,
That we may learn to bear the beams of love,
And these black bodies and this sun-burnt face
Is but a cloud, and like a shady grove.

For when our souls have learn'd the heat to bear
The cloud will vanish we shall hear his voice.
Saying: come out from the grove my love & care,
And round my golden tent like lambs rejoice.

Thus did my mother say and kissed me,
And thus I say to little English boy.
When I from black and he from white cloud free,
And round the tent of God like lambs we joy:

Ill shade him from the heat till he can bear,
To lean in joy upon our fathers knee.
And then I'll stand and stroke his silver hair,
And be like him and he will then love me.

The Divine Image

To Mercy Pity Peace and Love,
All pray in their distress:
And to these virtues of delight
Return their thankfulness.

For Mercy Pity Peace and Love,
Is God our father dear:
And Mercy Pity Peace and Love,
Is Man his child and care.

For Mercy has a human heart
Pity, a human face:
And Love, the human form divine,
And Peace, the human dress.

Then every man of every clime,
That prays in his distress,
Prays to the human form divine
Love Mercy Pity Peace.

And all must love the human form,
In heathen, turk or jew.
Where Mercy, Love & Pity dwell,
There God is dwelling too.

Holy Thursday

Twas on a Holy Thursday their innocent faces clean
The children walking two & two in red & blue & green
Grey headed beadles walkd before with wands as white as snow
Till into the high dome of Pauls they like Thames waters flow

O what a multitude they seemd these flowers of London town
Seated in companies they sit with radiance all their own
The hum of multitudes was there but multitudes of lambs
Thousands of little boys & girls raising their innocent hands

Now like a mighty wind they raise to heaven the voice of song
Or like harmonious thunderings the seats of heaven among
Beneath them sit the aged men wise guardians of the poor
Then cherish pity, lest you drive an angel from your door.

The Chimney Sweeper

When my mother died I was very young,
And my father sold me while yet my tongue,
Could scarcely cry " 'weep 'weep 'weep 'weep".
So your chimneys I sweep & in soot I sleep.

Theres little Tom Dacre, who cried when his head
That curl'd like a lambs back, was shav'd, so I said.
Hush Tom never mind it, for when your head's bare,
You know that the soot cannot spoil your white hair.

And so he was quiet, & that very night,
As Tom was a sleeping he had such a sight,
That thousands of sweepers Dick, Joe, Ned & Jack
Were all of them lock'd up in coffins of black,

And by came an Angel who had a bright key,
And he open'd the coffins & set them all free.
Then down a green plain leaping laughing they run
And wash in a river and shine in the Sun.

Then naked & white, all their bags left behind,
They rise upon clouds, and sport in the wind.
And the Angel told Tom if he'd be a good boy,
He'd have God for his father & never want joy.

And so Tom awoke and we rose in the dark
And got with our bags & our brushes to work.
Tho' the morning was cold, Tom was happy & warm,
So if all do their duty, they need not fear harm.

A Dream

Once a dream did weave a shade,
O'er my Angel-guarded bed,
That an Emmet lost it's way
Where on grass methought I lay.

Troubled wilderd and folorn
Dark benighted travel-worn,
Over many a tangled spray
All heart-broke I heard her say.

O my children! do they cry
Do they hear their father sigh.
Now they look abroad to see,
Now return and weep for me.

Pitying I drop'd a tear:
But I saw a glow-worm near:
Who replied. What wailing wight
Calls the watchman of the night.

I am set to light the ground,
While the beetle goes his round:
Follow now the beetles hum,
Little wanderer hie thee home.

On Anothers Sorrow

Can I see anothers woe,
And not be in sorrow too.
Can I see anothers grief,
And not seek for kind relief.

Can I see a falling tear,
And not feel my sorrows share,
Can a father see his child,
Weep, nor be with sorrow fill'd.

Can a mother sit and hear,
An infant groan an infant fear –
No no never can it be.
Never never can it be.

And can he who smiles on all
Hear the wren with sorrows small,
Hear the small birds grief & care
Hear the woes that infants bear –

And not sit beside the nest
Pouring pity in their breast,
And not sit the cradle near
Weeping tear on infants tear.

And not sit both night & day,
Wiping all our tears away.
O! no never can it be.
Never never can it be.

He doth give his joy to all.
He becomes an infant small.
He becomes a man of woe
He doth feel the sorrow too.

Think not, thou canst sigh a sigh,
And thy maker is not by.
Think not, thou canst weep a tear,
And thy maker is not near.

O! he gives to us his joy,
That our grief he may destroy
Till our grief is fled & gone
He doth sit by us and moan.

Poems from *Songs of Experience*

The Clod and the Pebble

Love seeketh not Itself to please,
Nor for itself hath any care;
But for another gives its ease,
And builds a Heaven in Hells despair.

So sang a little Clod of Clay,
Trodden with the cattles feet:
But a Pebble of the brook,
Warbled out these metres meet.

Love seeketh only Self to please,
To bind another to Its delight:
Joys in anothers loss of ease,
And builds a Hell in Heavens despite.

London

I wander thro' each charter'd street,
Near where the charter'd Thames does flow.
And mark in every face I meet
Marks of weakness, marks of woe.

In every cry of every Man,
In every Infants cry of fear,
In every voice: in every ban,
The mind-forg'd manacles I hear

How the Chimney-sweepers cry
Every blackning Church appalls,
And the hapless Soldiers sigh
Runs in blood down Palace walls

But most thro' midnight streets I hear
How the youthful Harlots curse
Blasts the new-born Infants tear
And blights with plagues the Marriage hearse.

Infant Sorrow

My mother groand! my father wept.
Into the dangerous world I leapt:
Helpless, naked, piping loud;
Like a fiend hid in a cloud.

Struggling in my fathers hands:
Striving against my swadling bands:
Bound and weary I thought best
To sulk upon my mothers breast.

Nurse's Song

When the voices of children, are heard on the green
And whisprings are in the dale:
The days of my youth rise fresh in my mind,
My face turns green and pale.

Then come home my children, the sun is gone down
And the dews of night arise
Your spring & your day, are wasted in play
And your winter and night in disguise.

The Sick Rose

O Rose thou art sick.
The invisible worm,
That flies in the night
In the howling storm:

Has found out thy bed
Of crimson joy:
And his dark secret love
Does thy life destroy.

The Fly

Little Fly
Thy summers play,
My thoughtless hand
Has brush'd away.

Am not I
A fly like thee?
Or art not thou
A man like me?

For I dance
And drink & sing:
Till some blind hand
Shall brush my wing.

If thought is life
And strength & breath:
And the want
Of thought is death;

Then am I
A happy fly,
If I live,
Or if I die.

Ah! Sun-flower

Ah Sun-flower! weary of time,
Who countest the steps of the Sun:
Seeking after that sweet golden clime
Where the travellers journey is done.

Where the Youth pined away with desire,
And the pale Virgin shrouded in snow:
Arise from their graves and aspire,
Where my Sun-flower wishes to go.

The Tyger

Tyger Tyger, burning bright,
In the forests of the night;
What immortal hand or eye,
Could frame thy fearful symmetry?

In what distant deeps or skies.
Burnt the fire of thine eyes?
On what wings dare he aspire?
What the hand, dare sieze the fire?

And what shoulder, & what art,
Could twist the sinews of thy heart?
And when thy heart began to beat,
What dread hand? & what dread feet?

What the hammer? what the chain,
In what furnace was thy brain?
What the anvil? what dread grasp,
Dare its deadly terrors clasp!

When the stars threw down their spears
And water'd heaven with their tears:
Did he smile his work to see?
Did he who made the Lamb make thee?

Tyger Tyger burning bright,
In the forests of the night:
What immortal hand or eye,
Dare frame thy fearful symmetry?

A Poison Tree

I was angry with my friend;
I told my wrath, my wrath did end.
I was angry with my foe:
I told it not, my wrath did grow.

And I waterd it in fears,
Night & morning with my tears:
And I sunned it with smiles,
And with soft deceitful wiles.

And it grew both day and night.
Till it bore an apple bright.
And my foe beheld it shine,
And he knew that it was mine.

And into my garden stole,
When the night had veild the pole;
In the morning glad I see;
My foe outstretchd beneath the tree.

'Proverbs of Hell' from *The Marriage of Heaven and Hell*

In seed time learn, in harvest teach, in winter enjoy.

Drive your cart and your plow over the bones of the dead.

The road of excess leads to the palace of wisdom.

Prudence is a rich ugly old maid courted by Incapacity.

He who desires but acts not, breeds pestilence.

The cut worm forgives the plow.

Dip him in the river who loves water.

A fool sees not the same tree that a wise man sees.

He whose face gives no light, shall never become a star.

Eternity is in love with the productions of time.

The busy bee has no time for sorrow.

The hours of folly are measur'd by the clock, but of wisdom: no clock
can measure.

All wholsom food is caught without a net or a trap.

Bring out number weight & measure in a year of dearth.

No bird soars too high. if he soars with his own wings.

A dead body. revenges not injuries.

The most sublime act is to set another before you.

If the fool would persist in his folly he would become wise.
Folly is the cloke of knavery.

Shame is Prides cloke.

Prisons are built with stones of Law, Brothels with bricks of Religion.

The pride of the peacock is the glory of God.
The lust of the goat is the bounty of God.

The wrath of the lion is the wisdom of God.
The nakedness of woman is the work of God.

Excess of sorrow laughs. Excess of joy weeps.

The roaring of lions, the howling of wolves, the raging of the stormy sea, and the destructive sword. are portions of eternity too great for the eye of man.

The fox condemns the trap, not himself.

Joys impregnate. Sorrows bring forth.

Let man wear the fell of the lion. woman the fleece of the sheep.

The bird a nest, the spider a web, man friendship.

The selfish smiling fool. & the sullen frowning fool. shall be both thought wise. that they may be a rod.

What is now proved was once, only imagin'd.

The rat, the mouse, the fox, the rabbet; watch the roots, the lion, the tyger, the horse, the elephant, watch the fruits.

The cistern contains: the fountain overflows.

One thought. fills immensity.

Always be ready to speak your mind, and a base man will avoid you.

Every thing possible to be believ'd is an image of truth.

The eagle never lost so much time. as when he submitted to learn of the crow.

The fox provides for himself. but God provides for the lion.

Think in the morning, Act in the noon, Eat in the evening, Sleep in the night.

He who has sufferd you to impose on him knows you.

As the plow follows words, so God rewards prayers.

The tygers of wrath are wiser than the horses of instruction.

Expect poison from the standing water.

You never know what is enough unless you know what is more than enough.

Listen to the fools reproach! it is a kingly title!

The eyes of fire, the nostrils of air, the mouth of water, the beard of earth.

The weak in courage is strong in cunning.

The apple tree never asks the beech how he shall grow, nor the lion. the horse; how he shall take his prey.

The thankful reciever bears a plentiful harvest.

If others had not been foolish. we should be so.

The soul of sweet delight. can never be defil'd.

When thou seest an Eagle, thou seest a portion of Genius. lift up thy head!

As the catterpiller chooses the fairest leaves to lay her eggs on, so the priest lays his curse on the fairest joys.

To create a little flower is the labour of ages.

Damn. braces: Bless relaxes.

The best wine is the oldest. the best water the newest.

Prayers plow not! Praises reap not!
Joys laugh not! Sorrows weep not!

The head Sublime, the heart Pathos, the genitals Beauty, the hands & feet Proportion.

As the air to a bird or the sea to a fish, so is contempt to the contemptible.

The crow wish'd every thing was black, the owl, that every thing was white.

Exuberance is Beauty.

If the lion was advised by the fox. he would be cunning.

Improvement makes strait roads, but the crooked roads without Improvement, are roads of Genius.

Sooner murder an infant in its cradle than nurse unacted desires.

Where man is not nature is barren.

Truth can never be told so as to be understood, and not be believ'd.

Enough! or Too much.

The speech of the Archbishop of Paris from *The French Revolution*

Hearken, Monarch of France, to the terrors of heaven, and let thy soul drink of my counsel;
Sleeping at midnight in my golden tower, the repose of the labours of men
Wav'd its solemn cloud over my head. I awoke; a cold hand passed over my limbs, and behold
An aged form, white as snow, hov'ring in mist, weeping in the uncertain light,
Dim the form almost faded, tears fell down the shady cheeks; at his feet many cloth'd
In white robes, strewn in air censers and harps, silent they lay prostrated;
Beneath, in the awful void, myriads descending and weeping thro' dismal winds,
Endless the shady train shiv'ring descended, from the gloom where the aged form wept.
At length, trembling, the vision sighing, in a low voice, like the voice of the grasshopper whisper'd:
My groaning is heard in the abbeys, and God, so long worshipp'd, departs as a lamp
Without oil; for a curse is heard hoarse thro' the land, from a godless race
Descending to beasts; they look downward and labour and forget my holy law;
The sound of prayer fails from lips of flesh, and the holy hymn from thicken'd tongues;
For the bars of Chaos are burst; her millions prepare their fiery way
Thro' the orbed abode of the holy dead, to root up and pull down and remove,
And Nobles and Clergy shall fail from before me, and my cloud and vision be no more;
The mitre become black, the crown vanish, and the scepter and ivory staff
Of the ruler wither among bones of death; they shall consume from the thistly field,

And the sound of the bell, and voice of the sabbath, and singing of the holy choir,
Is turn'd into songs of the harlot in day, and cries of the virgin in night.
They shall drop at the plow and faint at the harrow, unredeem'd, unconfess'd, unpardon'd;
The priest rot in his surplice by the lawless lover, the holy beside the accursed,
The King, frowning in purple, beside the grey plowman, and their worms embrace together.

Three laments from *Visions of the Daughters of Albion*

I

Why does my Theotormon sit weeping upon the threshold;
And Oothoon hovers by his side, perswading him in vain:
I cry arise O Theotormon for the village dog
Barks at the breaking day. the nightingale has done lamenting.
The lark does rustle in the ripe corn, and the Eagle returns
From nightly prey, and lifts his golden beak to the pure east;
Shaking the dust from his immortal pinions to awake
The sun that sleeps too long. Arise my Theotormon I am pure.
Because the night is gone that clos'd me in its deadly black.
They told me that the night & day were all that I could see;
They told me that I had five senses to inclose me up.
And they inclos'd my infinite brain into a narrow circle.
And sunk my heart into the Abyss, a red round globe hot burning
Till all from life I was obliterated and erased.
Instead of morn arises a bright shadow, like an eye
In the eastern cloud: instead of night a sickly charnel house;
That Theotormon hears me not! to him the night and morn
Are both alike: a night of sighs, a morning of fresh tears;
And none but Bromion can hear my lamentations.

With what sense is it that the chicken shuns the ravenous hawk?
With what sense does the tame pigeon measure out the expanse?
With what sense does the bee form cells? have not the mouse & frog
Eyes and ears and sense of touch? yet are their habitations.
And their pursuits, as different as their forms and as their joys:
Ask the wild ass why he refuses burdens: and the meek camel
Why he loves man: is it because of eye ear mouth or skin
Or breathing nostrils? No. for these the wolf and tyger have.
Ask the blind worm the secrets of the grave, and why her spires
Love to curl round the bones of death; and ask the rav'nous snake
Where she gets poison: & the wing'd eagle why he loves the sun
And then tell me the thoughts of man, that have been hid of old.
Silent I hover all the night, and all day could be silent.
If Theotormon once would turn his loved eyes upon me;
How can I be defild when I reflect thy image pure?
Sweetest the fruit that the worm feeds on. & the soul prey'd on by woe
The new wash'd lamb ting'd with the village smoke & the bright swan

By the red earth of our immortal river: I bathe my wings.
And I am white and pure to hover round Theotormons breast.

II

Does not the great mouth laugh at a gift? & the narrow eyelids mock
At the labour that is above payment, and wilt thou take the ape
For thy councellor? or the dog, for a schoolmaster to thy children?
Does he who contemns poverty, and he who turns with abhorrence
From usury: feel the same passion or are they moved alike?
How can the giver of gifts experience the delights of the merchant?
How the industrious citizen the pains of the husbandman.
How different far the fat fed hireling with hollow drum;
Who buys whole corn fields into wastes, and sings upon the heath:
How different their eye and ear! how different the world to them!
With what sense does the parson claim the labour of the farmer?
What are his nets & gins & traps. & how does he surround him
With cold floods of abstraction, and with forests of solitude,
To build him castles and high spires. where kings & priests may dwell.
Till she who burns with youth. and knows no fixed lot; is bound
In spells of law to one she loaths: and must she drag the chain
Of life, in weary lust! must chilling murderous thoughts. obscure
The clear heaven of her eternal spring? to bear the wintry rage
Of a harsh terror driv'n to madness, bound to hold a rod
Over her shrinking shoulders all the day; & all the night
To turn the wheel of false desire: and longings that wake her womb
To the abhorred birth of cherubs in the human form
That live a pestilence & die a meteor & are no more.
Till the child dwell with one he hates. and do the deed he loaths
And the impure scourge force his seed into its unripe birth
E'er yet his eyelids can behold the arrows of the day.

Does the whale worship at thy footsteps as the hungry dog?
Or does he scent the mountain prey, because his nostrils wide
Draw in the ocean? does his eye discern the flying cloud
As the ravens eye? or does he measure the expanse like the vulture?
Does the still spider view the cliffs where eagles hide their young?
Or does the fly rejoice. because the harvest is brought in?
Does not the eagle scorn the earth & despise the treasures beneath?
But the mole knoweth what is there, & the worm shall tell it thee.
Does not the worm erect a pillar in the mouldering church yard?
And a palace of eternity in the jaws of the hungry grave

Over his porch these words are written. Take thy bliss O Man!
And sweet shall be thy taste & sweet thy infant joys renew!

III

The moment of desire! the moment of desire! The virgin
That pines for man; shall awaken her womb to enormous joys
In the secret shadows of her chamber; the youth shut up from
The lustful joy. shall forget to generate. & create an amorous image
In the shadows of his curtains and in the folds of his silent pillow.
Are not these the places of religion? the rewards of continence?
The self enjoyings of self denial? Why dost thou seek religion?
Is it because acts are not lovely, that thou seekest solitude,
Where the horrible darkness is impressed with reflections of desire.

A prophecy of freedom from *America*

The morning comes, the night decays, the watchmen leave their
stations;
The grave is burst, the spices shed, the linen wrapped up;
The bones of death, the cov'ring clay, the sinews shrunk & dry'd.
Reviving shake, inspiring move, breathing! awakening!
Spring like redeemed captives when their bonds & bars are burst;
Let the slave grinding at the mill, run out into the field:
Let him look up into the heavens & laugh in the bright air;
Let the inchained soul shut up in darkness and in sighing,
Whose face has never seen a smile in thirty weary years;
Rise and look out, his chains are loose, his dungeon doors are open.
And let his wife and children return from the opressors scourge;
They look behind at every step & believe it is a dream.
Singing. The Sun has left his blackness, & has found a fresher morning
And the fair Moon rejoices in the clear & cloudless night;
For Empire is no more, and now the Lion & Wolf shall cease.

Pandemonium from *America*

In the flames stood & view'd the armies drawn out in the sky
Washington Franklin Paine & Warren Allen Gates & Lee:
And heard the voice of Albions Angel give the thunderous command:
His plagues obedient to his voice flew forth out of their clouds
Falling upon America, as a storm to cut them off
As a blight cuts the tender corn when it begins to appear.
Dark is the heaven above, & cold & hard the earth beneath;
And as a plague wind fill'd with insects cuts off man & beast;
And as a sea o'erwhelms a land in the day of an earthquake;
Fury! rage! madness! in a wind swept through America
And the red flames of Orc that folded roaring fierce around
The angry shores, and the fierce rushing of th'inhabitants together:
The citizens of New-York close their books & lock their chests;
The mariners of Boston drop their anchors and unlade;
The scribe of Pensylvania casts his pen upon the earth;
The builder of Virginia throws his hammer down in fear.
Then had America been lost, o'erwhelm'd by the Atlantic,
And Earth had lost another portion of the infinite,
But all rush together in the night in wrath and raging fire
The red fires rag'd! the plagues recoil'd! then rolld they back with fury.

The introduction to *Europe*

Five windows light the cavern'd Man; thro' one he breathes the air;
Thro' one, hears music of the spheres; thro' one, the eternal vine
Flourishes, that he may recieve the grapes; thro' one can look.
And see small portions of the eternal world that ever groweth;
Thro' one, himself pass out what time he please, but he will not;
For stolen joys are sweet, & bread eaten in secret pleasant.

So sang a Fairy mocking as he sat on a streak'd Tulip,
Thinking none saw him: when he ceas'd I started from the trees!
And caught him in my hat as boys knock down a butterfly.
How know you this said I small Sir? where did you learn this song?
Seeing himself in my possession thus he answered me:
My master, I am yours. command me, for I must obey.

Then tell me, what is the material world, and is it dead?
He laughing answer'd: I will write a book on leaves of flowers,
If you will feed me on love-thoughts, & give me now and then
A cup of sparkling poetic fancies; so when I am tipsie,
I'll sing to you to this soft lute; and shew you all alive
The world, when every particle of dust breathes forth its joy.

I took him home in my warm bosom: as we went along
Wild flowers I gatherd; & he shew'd me each eternal flower:
He laugh'd aloud to see them whimper because they were pluck'd.
They hover'd round me like a cloud of incense: when I came
Into my parlour and sat down, and took my pen to write:
My Fairy sat upon the table, and dictated EUROPE.

Two prison scenes from *Europe*

I

Thought chang'd the infinite to a serpent; that which pitieth:
To a devouring flame; and man fled from its face and hid
In forests of night; then all the eternal forests were divided
Into earths rolling in circles of space, that like an ocean rush'd
And overwhelmed all except this finite wall of flesh.
Then was the serpent temple form'd, image of infinite
Shut up in finite revolutions, and man became an Angel;
Heaven a mighty circle turning; God a tyrant crown'd.

II

Enitharmon laugh'd in her sleep to see (O womans triumph)
Every house a den, every man bound; the shadows are filld
With spectres, and the windows wove over with curses of iron:
Over the doors Thou shalt not; & over the chimneys Fear is written:
With bands of iron round their necks fasten'd into the walls
The citizens: in leaden gyves the inhabitants of suburbs
Walk heavy: soft and bent are the bones of villagers.

Visions of despair from *The Song of Los*

I

The human race began to wither, for the healthy built
Secluded places, fearing the joys of Love
And the disease'd only propagated:
So Antamon call'd up Leutha from her valleys of delight:
And to Mahomet a loose Bible gave.
But in the North, to Odin, Sotha gave a Code of War,
Because of Diralada thinking to reclaim his joy.
These were the Churches: Hospitals: Castles: Palaces:
Like nets & gins & traps to catch the joys of Eternity
    And all the rest a desart;
Till like a dream Eternity was obliterated & erased.

II

Shall not the King call for Famine from the heath?
Nor the Priest, for Pestilence from the fen?
To restrain! to dismay! to thin!
The inhabitants of mountain and plain;
In the day, of full-feeding prosperity;
And the night of delicious songs.

Shall not the Councellor throw his curb
Of Poverty on the laborious?
To fix the price of labour;
To invent allegoric riches:
And the privy admonishers of men
Call for fires in the City
For heaps of smoking ruins,
In the night of prosperity & wantonness
To turn man from his path,
To restrain the child from the womb,
To cut off the bread from the city,
That the remnant may learn to obey.
That the pride of the heart may fail;
That the lust of the eyes may be quench'd:
That the delicate ear in its infancy

May be dull'd; and the nostrils clos'd up;
To teach mortal worms the path
That leads from the gates of the Grave.

Scenes from the life of Urizen from *The Book of Urizen*

I

Here alone I in books formd of metals
Have written the secrets of wisdom
The secrets of dark contemplation
By fightings and conflicts dire,
With terrible monsters Sin-bred:
Which the bosoms of all inhabit;
Seven deadly Sins of the soul.

Lo! I unfold my darkness: and on
This rock, place with strong hand the Book
Of eternal brass, written in my solitude.

Laws of peace, of love, of unity:
Of pity, compassion, forgiveness.
Let each chuse one habitation:
His ancient infinite mansion:
One command, one joy, one desire,
One curse, one weight, one measure
One King, one God, one Law.

II

Forgetfulness, dumbness, necessity!
In chains of the mind locked up,
Like fetters of ice shrinking together
Disorganiz'd, rent from Eternity,
Los beat on his fetters of iron;
And heated his furnaces & pour'd
Iron sodor and sodor of brass

Restless turnd the immortal inchain'd
Heaving dolorous! anguish'd! unbearable
Till a roof shaggy wild inclos'd
In an orb, his fountain of thought.

In a horrible dreamful slumber;
Like the linked infernal chain;
A vast Spine writh'd in torment
Upon the winds; shooting pain'd

Ribs, like a bending cavern
And bones of solidness, froze
Over all his nerves of joy.
And a first Age passed over,
And a state of dismal woe.

From the caverns of his jointed Spine,
Down sunk with fright a red
Round globe hot burning deep
Deep down into the Abyss:
Panting: Conglobing, Trembling
Shooting out ten thousand branches
Around his solid bones.
And a second Age passed over,
And a state of dismal woe.

In harrowing fear rolling round;
His nervous brain shot branches
Round the branches of his heart.
On high into two little orbs
And fixed in two little caves
Hiding carefully from the wind,
His Eyes beheld the deep,
And a third Age passed over:
And a state of dismal woe.

The pangs of hope began,
In heavy pain striving, struggling.
Two Ears in close volutions.
From beneath his orbs of vision
Shot spiring out and petrified
As they grew. And a fourth Age passed
And a state of dismal woe.

In ghastly torment sick;
Hanging upon the wind;
Two Nostrils bent down to the deep.
And a fifth Age passed over;
And a state of dismal woe.

In ghastly torment sick;
Within his ribs bloated round,
A craving Hungry Cavern;
Thence arose his channeld Throat,

And like a red flame a Tongue
Of thirst & hunger appeard.
And a sixth Age passed over:
And a state of dismal woe.

Enraged & stifled with torment
He threw his right Arm to the north
His left Arm to the south
Shooting out in anguish deep,
And his Feet stampd the nether Abyss
In trembling & howling & dismay.
And a seventh Age passed over:
And a state of dismal woe.

III

He form'd a line & a plummet
To divide the Abyss beneath.
He form'd a dividing rule:

He formed scales to weigh;
He formed massy weights;
He formed a brazen quadrant;

He formed golden compasses
And began to explore the Abyss
And he planted a garden of fruits.

IV

He in darkness clos'd, view'd all his race
And his soul sicken'd! he curs'd
Both sons & daughters; for he saw
That no flesh nor spirit could keep
His iron laws one moment.

For he saw that life liv'd upon death
The Ox in the slaughter house moans
The Dog at the wintry door
And he wept, & he called it Pity
And his tears flowed down on the winds

Cold he wander'd on high, over their cities
In weeping & pain & woe!

And where-ever he wanderd in sorrows
Upon the aged heavens
A cold shadow follow'd behind him
Like a spiders web, moist, cold, & dim
Drawing out from his sorrowing soul
The dungeon-like heaven dividing.
Where ever the footsteps of Urizen
Walk'd over the cities in sorrow.

Till a Web dark & cold, throughout all
The tormented element stretch'd
From the sorrows of Urizens soul
And the Web is a Female in embrio
None could break the Web, no wings of fire.
So twisted the cords, & so knotted
The meshes: twisted like to the human brain
And all calld it, The Net of Religion.

The preface to *Milton*

And did those feet in ancient time,
Walk upon Englands mountains green:
And was the holy Lamb of God,
On Englands pleasant pastures seen!

And did the Countenance Divine,
Shine forth upon our clouded hills?
And was Jerusalem builded here,
Among these dark Satanic Mills?

Bring me my Bow of burning gold:
Bring me my Arrows of desire:
Bring me my Spear: O clouds unfold!
Bring me my Chariot of fire!

I will not cease from Mental Fight,
Nor shall my Sword sleep in my hand:
Till we have built Jerusalem,
In Englands green & pleasant Land.

Scenes from *Milton*

I

Ah weak & wide astray! Ah shut in narrow doleful form
Creeping in reptile flesh upon the bosom of the ground
The Eye of Man a little narrow orb closd up & dark
Scarcely beholding the great light conversing with the Void
The Ear, a little shell in small volutions shutting out
All melodies & comprehending only Discord and Harmony
The Tongue a little moisture fills, a little food it cloys
A little sound it utters & its cries are faintly heard
Then brings forth Moral Virtue the cruel Virgin Babylon

Can such an Eye judge of the stars? & looking thro its tubes
Measure the sunny rays that point their spears on Udanadan
Can such an Ear filld with the vapours of the yawning pit.
Judge of the pure melodious harp struck by a hand divine?
Can such closed Nostrils feel a joy? or tell of autumn fruits
When grapes & figs burst their covering to the joyful air
Can such a Tongue boast of the living waters? or take in
Ought but the Vegetable Ratio & loathe the faint delight
Can such gross Lips percieve? alas! folded within themselves
They touch not ought but pallid turn & tremble at every wind.

II

The nature of infinity is this: That every thing has its
Own Vortex; and when once a traveller thro Eternity.
Has passd that Vortex, he percieves it roll backward behind
His path, into a globe itself infolding; like a sun:
Or like a moon, or like a universe of starry majesty,
While he keeps onwards in his wondrous journey on the earth
Or like a human form, a friend with whom he livd benevolent.
As the eye of man views both the east & west encompassing
Its vortex; and the north & south, with all their starry host;
Also the rising sun & setting moon he views surrounding
His corn-fields and his valleys of five hundred acres square.
Thus is the earth one infinite plane, and not as apparent
To the weak traveller confin'd beneath the moony shade.
Thus is the heaven a vortex passd already, and the earth
A vortex not yet pass'd by the traveller thro' Eternity.

First Milton saw Albion upon the Rock of Ages,
Deadly pale outstretchd and snowy cold, storm coverd;
A Giant form of perfect beauty outstretchd on the rock
In solemn death: the Sea of Time & Space thunderd aloud
Against the rock, which was inwrapped with the weeds of death
Hovering over the cold bosom, in its vortex Milton bent down
To the bosom of death, what was underneath soon seemd above.
A cloudy heaven mingled with stormy seas in loudest ruin;
But as a wintry globe descends precipitant thro' Beulah bursting,
With thunders loud and terrible: so Miltons shadow fell
Precipitant loud thundring into the Sea of Time & Space.

Then first I saw him in the Zenith as a falling star,
Descending perpendicular, swift as the swallow or swift;
And on my left foot falling on the tarsus, enterd there;
But from my left foot a black cloud redounding spread over Europe.

III

I will lament over Milton in the lamentations of the afflicted
My Garments shall be woven of sighs & heart broken lamentations
The misery of unhappy Families shall be drawn out into its border
Wrought with the needle with dire sufferings poverty pain & woe
Along the rocky Island & thence throughout the whole Earth
There shall be the sick Father & his starving Family! there
The Prisoner in the stone Dungeon & the Slave at the Mill
I will have Writings written all over it in Human Words
That every Infant that is born upon the Earth shall read
And get by rote as a hard task of a life of sixty years
I will have Kings inwoven upon it, & Councellors & Mighty Men
The Famine shall clasp it together with buckles & Clasps
And the Pestilence shall be its fringe & the War its girdle
To divide into Rahab & Tirzah that Milton may come to our tents
For I will put on the Human Form & take the Image of God
Even Pity & Humanity but my Clothing shall be Cruelty
And I will put on Holiness as a breastplate & as a helmet
And all my ornaments shall be of the gold of broken hearts
And the precious stones of anxiety & care & desperation & death
And repentance for sin & sorrow & punishment & fear
To defend me from thy terrors O Orc! my only beloved!

IV

Now Albions sleeping Humanity began to turn upon his Couch;
Feeling the electric flame of Miltons awful precipitate descent.
Seest thou the little winged fly, smaller than a grain of sand?
It has a heart like thee; a brain open to heaven & hell,
Withinside wondrous & expansive; its gates are not clos'd,
I hope thine are not: hence it clothes itself in rich array;
Hence thou art cloth'd with human beauty O thou mortal man.
Seek not thy heavenly father then beyond the skies.

V

I am that Shadowy Prophet who Six Thousand Years ago
Fell from my station in the Eternal bosom. Six Thousand Years
Are finishd. I return! both Time & Space obey my will.
I in Six Thousand Years walk up and down: for not one Moment
Of Time is lost, nor one Event of Space unpermanent
But all remain: every fabric of Six Thousand Years
Remains permanent: tho' on the Earth where Satan
Fell, and was cut off all things vanish & are seen no more
They vanish not from me & mine, we guard them first & last
The generations of men run on in the tide of Time
But leave their destind lineaments permanent for ever & ever.

VI

And Los thus spoke. O noble Sons, be patient yet a little
I have embracd the falling Death, he is become One with me
O Sons we live not by wrath. by mercy alone we live!
I recollect an old Prophecy in Eden recorded in gold; and oft
Sung to the harp: That Milton of the land of Albion.
Should up ascend forward from Felphams Vale & break the Chain
Of Jealousy from all its roots; be patient therefore O my Sons
These lovely Females form sweet night and silence and secret
Obscurities to hide from Satans Watch-Fiends. Human loves
And graces; lest they write them in their Books, & in the Scroll
Of mortal life, to condemn the accused: who at Satans Bar
Tremble in Spectrous Bodies continually day and night
While on the Earth they live in sorrowful Vegetations
O when shall we tread our Wine-presses in heaven; and Reap
Our wheat with shoutings of joy, and leave the Earth in peace

Remember how Calvin and Luther in fury premature
Sow'd War and stern division between Papists & Protestants
Let it not be so now! O go not forth in Martyrdoms & Wars
We were plac'd here by the Universal Brotherhood & Mercy
With powers fitted to circumscribe this dark Satanic death
And that the Seven Eyes of God may have space for Redemption.
But how this is as yet we know not, and we cannot know;
Till Albion is arisen; then patient wait a little while,
Six Thousand years are passd away the end approaches fast;
This mighty one is come from Eden, he is of the Elect,
Who died from Earth & he is returnd before the Judgment. This thing
Was never known that one of the holy dead should willing return
Then patient wait a little while till the Last Vintage is over.

VII

Fellow Labourers! The Great Vintage & Harvest is now upon Earth
The whole extent of the Globe is explored: Every scatterd Atom
Of Human Intellect now is flocking to the sound of the Trumpet
All the Wisdom which was hidden in caves & dens, from ancient
Time; is now sought out from Animal & Vegetable & Mineral
The Awakener is come, outstretchd over Europe! the Vision of God is
fulfilled
The Ancient Man upon the Rock of Albion Awakes.

VIII

Thou seest the Constellations in the deep & wondrous Night
They rise in order and continue their immortal courses
Upon the mountains & in vales with harp & heavenly song
With flute & clarion; with cups & measures filld with foaming wine.
Glittring the streams reflect the Vision of beatitude,
And the calm Ocean joys beneath & smooths his awful waves!
These are the Sons of Los, & these the Labourers of the Vintage
Thou seest the gorgeous clothed Flies that dance & sport in summer
Upon the sunny brooks & meadows: every one the dance
Knows in its intricate mazes of delight artful to weave:
Each one to sound his instruments of music in the dance,
To touch each other & recede; to cross & change & return
These are the Children of Los; thou seest the Trees on mountains
The wind blows heavy, loud they thunder thro' the darksom sky
Uttering prophecies & speaking instructive words to the sons

Of men: These are the Sons of Los! These the Visions of Eternity
But we see only as it were the hem of their garments
When with our vegetable eyes we view these wond'rous Visions.

IX

And every Natural Effect has a Spiritual Cause, and Not
A Natural: for a Natural Cause only seems, it is a Delusion
Of Ulro: & a ratio of the perishing Vegetable Memory.

X

Timbrels & violins sport round the Wine-presses; the little Seed;
The sportive Root, the Earth-worm, the gold Beetle; the wise Emmet;
Dance round the Wine-presses of Luvah: the Centipede is there:
The ground Spider with many eyes: the Mole clothed in velvet
The ambitious Spider in his sullen web; the lucky golden Spinner;
The Earwig armd: the tender Maggot emblem of immortality:
The Flea: Louse: Bug: the Tape-Worm: all the Armies of Disease:
Visible or invisible to the slothful vegetating Man.
The slow Slug: the Grasshopper that sings & laughs & drinks:
Winter comes, he folds his slender bones without a murmur.
The cruel Scorpion is there: the Gnat: Wasp: Hornet & the Honey Bee:
The Toad & venomous Newt; the Serpent clothd in gems & gold:
They throw off their gorgeous raiment: they rejoice with loud jubilee
Around the Wine-presses of Luvah, naked & drunk with wine.
There is the Nettle that stings with soft down; and there
The indignant Thistle: whose bitterness is bred in his milk:
Who feeds on contempt of his neighbour: there all the idle Weeds
That creep around the obscure places, shew their various limbs.
Naked in all their beauty dancing round the Wine-presses.

XI

Some Sons of Los surround the Passions with porches of iron & silver
Creating form & beauty around the dark regions of sorrow,
Giving to airy nothing a name and a habitation
Delightful! with bounds to the Infinite putting off the Indefinite
Into most holy forms of Thought: (such is the power of inspiration)
They labour incessant; with many tears & afflictions:
Creating the beautiful House for the piteous sufferer.

XII

The Sons of Ozoth within the Optic Nerve stand fiery glowing
And the number of his Sons is eight millions & eight.
They give delights to the man unknown; artificial riches
They give to scorn, & their posessors to trouble & sorrow & care,
Shutting the sun. & moon. & stars. & trees. & clouds. & waters.
And hills. out from the Optic Nerve & hardening it into a bone
Opake. and like the black pebble on the enraged beach.
While the poor indigent is like the diamond which tho cloth'd
In rugged covering in the mine, is open all within
And in his hallowd center holds the heavens of bright eternity
Ozoth here builds walls of rocks against the surging sea
And timbers crampt with iron cramps bar in the joys of life
From fell destruction in the Spectrous cunning or rage. He Creates
The speckled Newt, the Spider & Beetle, the Rat & Mouse,
The Badger & Fox: they worship before his feet in trembling fear.
But others of the Sons of Los build Moments & Minutes & Hours
And Days & Months & Years & Ages & Periods; wondrous buildings
And every Moment has a Couch of gold for soft repose,
(A Moment equals a pulsation of the artery)
And between every two Moments stands a Daughter of Beulah
To feed the Sleepers on their Couches with maternal care.
And every Minute has an azure Tent with silken Veils.
And every Hour has a bright golden Gate carved with skill.
And every Day & Night, has Walls of brass & Gates of adamant,
Shining like precious stones & ornamented with appropriate signs:
And every Month, a silver paved Terrace builded high:
And every Year, invulnerable Barriers with high Towers.
And every Age is Moated deep with Bridges of silver & gold.
And every Seven Ages is Incircled with a Flaming Fire.
Now Seven Ages is amounting to Two Hundred Years
Each has its Guard. each Moment Minute Hour Day Month & Year.
All are the work of Fairy hands of the Four Elements
The Guard are Angels of Providence on duty evermore
Every Time less than a pulsation of the artery
Is equal in its period & value to Six Thousand Years.
For in this Period the Poets Work is Done: and all the Great
Events of Time start forth & are concievd in such a Period
Within a Moment: a Pulsation of the Artery.

The Sky is an immortal Tent built by the Sons of Los
And every Space that a Man views around his dwelling-place:

Standing on his own roof, or in his garden on a mount
Of twenty-five cubits in height, such space is his Universe;
And on its verge the Sun rises & sets. the Clouds bow
To meet the flat Earth & the Sea in such an orderd Space:
The Starry heavens reach no further but here bend and set
On all sides & the two Poles turn on their valves of gold:
And if he move his dwelling-place, his heavens also move.
Wher'eer he goes & all his neighbourhood bewail his loss:
Such are the Spaces called Earth & such its dimension:
As to that false appearance which appears to the reasoner,
As of a Globe rolling thro Voidness, it is a delusion of Ulro
The Microscope knows not of this nor the Telescope. they alter
The ratio of the Spectators Organs but leave Objects untouchd
For every Space larger than a red Globule of Mans blood.
Is visionary: and is created by the Hammer of Los
And every Space smaller than a Globule of Mans blood. opens
Into Eternity of which this vegetable Earth is but a shadow:
The red Globule is the unwearied Sun by Los created
To measure Time and Space to mortal Men. every morning.
Bowlahoola & Allamanda are placed on each side
Of that Pulsation & that Globule, terrible their power.

XIII

Thou hearest the Nightingale begin the Song of Spring;
The Lark sitting upon his earthy bed: just as the morn
Appears; listens silent; then springing from the waving Corn-field! loud
He leads the Choir of Day! trill, trill, trill, trill,
Mounting upon the wings of light into the Great Expanse:
Reecchoing against the lovely blue & shining heavenly Shell:
His little throat labours with inspiration; every feather
On throat & breast & wings vibrates with the effluence Divine
All Nature listens silent to him & the awful Sun
Stands still upon the Mountain looking on this little Bird
With eyes of soft humility, & wonder love & awe.
Then loud from their green covert all the Birds begin their Song
The Thrush, the Linnet & the Goldfinch, Robin & the Wren
Awake the Sun from his Sweet reverie upon the Mountain:
The Nightingale again assays his song, & thro the day,
And thro the night warbles luxuriant; every Bird of Song
Attending his loud harmony with admiration & love.

This is a Vision of the lamentation of Beulah over Ololon!
Thou percievest the Flowers put forth their precious Odours!
And none can tell how from so small a center comes such sweets
Forgetting that within that Center Eternity expands
Its ever during doors, that Og & Anak fiercely guard
First eer the morning breaks joy opens in the flowery bosoms
Joy even to tears, which the Sun rising dries; first the Wild Thyme
And Meadow-sweet downy & soft waving among the reeds.
Light springing on the air lead the sweet Dance: they wake
The Honeysuckle sleeping on the Oak: the flaunting beauty
Revels along upon the wing; the White-thorn lovely May
Opens her many lovely eyes: listening the Rose still sleeps
None dare to wake her. soon she bursts her crimson curtaind bed
And comes forth in the majesty of beauty; every Flower:
The Pink, the Jessamine, the Wall-flower, the Carnation
The Jonquil, the mild Lilly opes her heavens! every Tree,
And Flower & Herb soon fill the air with an innumerable Dance
Yet all in order sweet & lovely, Men are sick with Love!
Such is a Vision of the lamentation of Beulah over Ololon.

XIV

The Imagination is not a State: it is the Human Existence itself
Affection or Love becomes a State, when divided from Imagination
The Memory is a State always, & the Reason is a State
Created to be Annihilated & a new Ratio Created
Whatever can be Created can be Annihilated Forms cannot
The Oak is cut down by the Ax, the Lamb falls by the Knife
But their Forms Eternal Exist, For-ever. Amen Hallelujah
Thus they converse with the Dead watching round the Couch of
    Death.
For God himself enters Death's Door always with those that enter
And lays down in the Grave with them, in Visions of Eternity
Till they awake & see Jesus & the Linen Clothes lying
That the Females had Woven for them, & the Gates of their Fathers
    House.

XV

There is a Moment in each Day that Satan cannot find
Nor can his Watch Fiends find it, but the Industrious find
This Moment & it multiply. & when it once is found

It renovates every Moment of the Day if rightly placed
In this Moment Ololon descended to Los & Enitharmon
Unseen beyond the Mundane Shell Southward in Miltons track.

XVI

I also stood in Satans bosom & beheld its desolations!
A ruind Man: a ruind building of God not made with hands;
Its plains of burning sand, its mountains of marble terrible:
Its pits & declivities flowing with molten ore & fountains
Of pitch & nitre: its ruind palaces & cities & mighty works;
Its furnaces of affliction in which his Angels & Emanations
Labour with blackend visages among its stupendous ruins
Arches & pyramids & porches colonades & domes:
In which dwells Mystery Babylon, here is her secret place
From hence she comes forth on the Churches in delight
Here is her Cup filld with its poisons, in these horrid vales
And here her scarlet Veil woven in pestilence & war:
Here is Jerusalem bound in chains, in the Dens of Babylon.

XVII

No sooner she had spoke but Rahab Babylon appeard
Eastward upon the Paved work across Europe & Asia
Glorious in the midday Sun in Satans bosom glowing:
A Female hidden in a Male, Religion hidden in War
Namd Moral Virtue; cruel two-fold Monster shining bright
A Dragon red & hidden Harlot which John in Patmos saw.

XVIII

To bathe in the Waters of Life; to wash off the Not Human
I come in Self-annihilation & the grandeur of Inspiration
To cast off Rational Demonstration by Faith in the Saviour
To cast off the rotten rags of Memory by Inspiration
To cast off Bacon, Locke & Newton from Albions covering
To take off his filthy garments, & clothe him with Imagination
To cast aside from Poetry, all that is not Inspiration
That it no longer shall dare to mock with the aspersion of Madness
Cast on the Inspired, by the tame high finisher of paltry Blots,
Indefinite, or paltry Rhymes; or paltry Harmonies.
Who creeps into State Government like a catterpiller to destroy

To cast off the idiot Questioner who is always questioning,
But never capable of answering; who sits with a sly grin
Silent plotting when to question, like a thief in a cave;
Who publishes doubt & calls it knowledge; whose Science is Despair
Whose pretence to knowledge is Envy, whose whole Science is
To destroy the wisdom of ages to gratify ravenous Envy;
That rages round him like a Wolf day & night without rest
He smiles with condescension; he talks of Benevolence & Virtue
And those who act with Benevolence & Virtue, they murder time on
time
These are the destroyers of Jerusalem, these are the murderers
Of Jesus, who deny the Faith & mock at Eternal Life:
Who pretend to Poetry that they may destroy Imagination;
By Imitation of Natures Images drawn from Remembrance
These are the Sexual Garments, the Abomination of Desolation
Hiding the Human Lineaments as with an Ark & Curtains
Which Jesus rent: & now shall wholly purge away with Fire
Till Generation is swallowd up in Regeneration.

XIX

Immediately the Lark mounted with a loud trill from Felphams Vale
And the Wild Thyme from Wimbletons green & impurpled Hills
And Los & Enitharmon rose over the Hills of Surrey
Their clouds roll over London with a south wind, soft Oothoon
Pants in the Vales of Lambeth weeping oer her Human Harvest
Los listens to the Cry of the Poor Man: his Cloud
Over London in volume terrific, low bended in anger.

Rintrah & Palamabron view the Human Harvest beneath
Their Wine-presses & Barns stand open; the Ovens are prepar'd
The Waggons ready: terrific Lions & Tygers sport & play
All Animals upon the Earth, are prepard in all their strength
To go forth to the Great Harvest & Vintage of the Nations.

Occasional verses

I

Eternity

He who binds to himself a joy
Does the winged life destroy
But he who kisses the joy as it flies
Lives in eternity's sun rise

II

O lapwing thou fliest around the heath
Nor seest the net that is spread beneath
Why dost thou not fly among the corn fields
They cannot spread nets where a harvest yields

III

If you trap the moment before its ripe
The tears of repentance youll certainly wipe
But if once you let the ripe moment go
You can never wipe off the tears of woe

IV

Merlins prophecy

The harvest shall flourish in wintry weather
When two virginities meet together

The King & the Priest must be tied in a tether
Before two virgins can meet together

V

The Vision of Christ that thou dost see
Is my Visions Greatest Enemy
Thine has a great hook nose like thine
Mine has a snub nose like to mine
Thine is the Friend of All Mankind
Mine speaks in parables to the Blind
Thine loves the same world that mine hates
Thy Heaven doors are my Hell Gates
Socrates taught what Melitus
Loathd as a Nations bitterest Curse
And Caiphas was in his own Mind
A benefactor of Mankind
Both read the Bible day & night
But thou readst black where I read white

VI

What is it men in women do require
The lineaments of Gratified Desire

What is it women do in men require
The lineaments of Gratified Desire

Preludes to *Jerusalem*

I

The fields from Islington to Marybone,
To Primrose Hill and Saint Johns Wood:
Were builded over with pillars of gold,
And there Jerusalems pillars stood.

Her Little-ones ran on the fields
The Lamb of God among them seen
And fair Jerusalem his Bride:
Among the little meadows green.

Pancrass & Kentish-town repose
Among her golden pillars high:
Among her golden arches which
Shine upon the starry sky.

The Jews-harp-house & the Green Man;
The Ponds where Boys to bathe delight:
The fields of Cows by Willans farm:
Shine in Jerusalems pleasant sight.

She walks upon our meadows green:
The Lamb of God walks by her side:
And every English Child is seen,
Children of Jesus & his Bride,

Forgiving trespasses and sins
Lest Babylon with cruel Og,
With Moral & Self-righteous Law
Should Crucify in Satans Synagogue!

What are those golden Builders doing
Near mournful ever-weeping Paddington
Standing above that mighty Ruin
Where Satan the first victory won.

Where Albion slept beneath the Fatal Tree
And the Druids golden Knife,
Rioted in human gore,
In Offerings of Human Life

They groan'd aloud on London Stone
They groan'd aloud on Tyburns Brook
Albion gave his deadly groan,
And all the Atlantic Mountains shook

Albions Spectre from his Loins
Tore forth in all the pomp of War!
Satan his name: in flames of fire
He stretch'd his Druid Pillars far.

Jerusalem fell from Lambeth's Vale,
Down thro Poplar & Old Bow;
Thro Malden & acros the Sea,
In War & howling death & woe.

The Rhine was red with human blood:
The Danube rolld a purple tide:
On the Euphrates Satan stood:
And over Asia stretch'd his pride.

He witherd up sweet Zions Hill,
From every Nation of the Earth:
He witherd up Jerusalems Gates,
And in a dark Land gave her birth.

He witherd up the Human Form,
By laws of sacrifice for sin:
Till it became a Mortal Worm:
But O! translucent all within.

The Divine Vision still was seen
Still was the Human Form, Divine
Weeping in weak & mortal clay
O Jesus still the Form was thine.

And thine the Human Face & thine
The Human Hands & Feet & Breath
Entering thro' the Gates of Birth
And passing thro' the Gates of Death

And O thou Lamb of God, whom I
Slew in my dark self-righteous pride:
Art thou return'd to Albions Land!
And is Jerusalem thy Bride?

Come to my arms & never more
Depart; but dwell for ever here:
Create my Spirit to thy Love:
Subdue my Spectre to thy Fear.

Spectre of Albion! warlike Fiend!
In clouds of blood & ruin roll'd:
I here reclaim thee as my own
My Selfhood! Satan! armd in gold.

Is this thy soft Family-Love
Thy cruel Patriarchal pride
Planting thy Family alone
Destroying all the World beside.

A mans worst enemies are those
Of his own house & family;
And he who makes his law a curse,
By his own law shall surely die.

In my Exchanges every Land
Shall walk, & mine in every Land,
Mutual shall build Jerusalem:
Both heart in heart & hand in hand.

II

I saw a Monk of Charlemaine
Arise before my sight
I talkd with the Grey Monk as we stood
In beams of infernal light

Gibbon arose with a lash of steel
And Voltaire with a wracking wheel
The Schools in clouds of learning rolld
Arose with War in iron & gold.

Thou lazy Monk they sound afar
In vain condemning glorious War
And in your Cell you shall ever dwell
Rise War & bind him in his Cell.

The blood. red ran from the Grey Monks side
His hands & feet were wounded wide

His body bent, his arms & knees
Like to the roots of ancient trees

When Satan first the black bow bent
And the Moral Law from the Gospel rent
He forgd the Law into a Sword
And spilld the blood of mercys Lord.

Titus! Constantine! Charlemaine!
O Voltaire! Rousseau! Gibbon! Vain
Your Grecian Mocks & Roman Sword
Against this image of his Lord!

For a Tear is an Intellectual thing;
And a Sigh is the Sword of an Angel King
And the bitter groan of a Martyrs woe
Is an Arrow from the Almighties Bow!

III

I give you the end of a golden string,
Only wind it into a ball:
It will lead you in at Heavens gate,
Built in Jerusalems wall.

Scenes from *Jerusalem*

I

The banks of the Thames are clouded! the ancient porches of Albion
are
Darken'd! they are drawn thro' unbounded space, scatter'd upon
The Void in incoherent despair! Cambridge & Oxford & London,
Are driven among the starry Wheels, rent away and dissipated,
In Chasms & Abysses of sorrow, enlarg'd without dimension, terrible
Albions mountains run with blood, the cries of war & of tumult
Resound into the unbounded night, every Human perfection
Of mountain & river & city, are small & wither'd & darken'd
Cam is a little stream! Ely is almost swallowd up!
Lincoln & Norwich stand trembling on the brink of Udan-Adan!
Wales and Scotland shrink themselves to the west and to the north!
Mourning for fear of the warriors in the Vale of Entuthon-Benython
Jerusalem is scatterd abroad like a cloud of smoke thro' non-entity:
Moab & Ammon & Amalek & Canaan & Egypt & Aram
Recieve her little-ones for sacrifices and the delights of cruelty
Trembling I sit day and night, my friends are astonish'd at me.
Yet they forgive my wanderings, I rest not from my great task!
To open the Eternal Worlds, to open the immortal Eyes
Of Man inwards into the Worlds of Thought: into Eternity
Ever expanding in the Bosom of God. the Human Imagination
O Saviour pour upon me thy Spirit of meekness & love:
Annihilate the Selfhood in me, be thou all my life!
Guide thou my hand which trembles exceedingly upon the rock of
ages.

II

I labour day and night, I behold the soft affections
Condense beneath my hammer into forms of cruelty
But still I labour in hope, tho' still my tears flow down.
That he who will not defend Truth, may be compelld to defend
A Lie: that he may be snared and caught and snared and taken
That Enthusiasm and Life may not cease: arise Spectre arise!

III

The Spectre answer'd. Art thou not ashamed of those thy Sins
That thou callest thy Children? lo the Law of God commands

That they be offered upon his Altar: O cruelty & torment
For thine are also mine! I have kept silent hitherto,
Concerning my chief delight: but thou hast broken silence
Now I will speak my mind! Where is my lovely Enitharmon
O thou my enemy, where is my Great Sin? She is also thine
I said: now is my grief at worst: incapable of being
Surpassed: but every moment it accumulates more & more
It continues accumulating to eternity! the joys of God advance
For he is Righteous: he is not a Being of Pity & Compassion
He cannot feel Distress: he feeds on Sacrifice & Offering:
Delighting in cries & tears & clothed in holiness & solitude
But my griefs advance also, for ever & ever without end
O that I could cease to be! Despair! I am Despair
Created to be the great example of horror & agony: also my
Prayer is vain I called for compassion: compassion mockd
Mercy & pity threw the grave stone over me & with lead
And iron, bound it over me for ever: Life lives on my
Consuming: & the Almighty hath made me his Contrary
To be all evil, all reversed & for ever dead: knowing
And seeing life, yet living not; how can I then behold
And not tremble; how can I be beheld & not abhorrd.

IV

What are those golden builders doing? where was the burying-place
Of soft Ethinthus? near Tyburns fatal Tree? is that
Mild Zions hills most ancient promontory; near mournful
Ever weeping Paddington? is that Calvary and Golgotha?
Becoming a building of pity and compassion? Lo!
The stones are pity, and the bricks, well wrought affections:
Enameld with love & kindness, & the tiles engraven gold
Labour of merciful hands: the beams & rafters are forgiveness:
The mortar & cement of the work, tears of honesty: the nails,
And the screws & iron braces, are well wrought blandishments,
And well contrived words, firm fixing, never forgotten,
Always comforting the remembrance: the floors, humility,
The cielings, devotion: the hearths, thanksgiving:
Prepare the furniture O Lambeth in thy pitying looms!
The curtains, woven tears & sighs, wrought into lovely forms
For comfort. there the secret furniture of Jerusalems chamber

Is wrought: Lambeth! the Bride the Lambs Wife loveth thee:
Thou art one with her & knowest not of self in thy supreme joy.
Go on, builders in hope: tho Jerusalem wanders far away,
Without the gate of Los: among the dark Satanic wheels.

V

There is the Cave; the Rock; the Tree; the Lake of Udan Adan;
The Forest, and the Marsh, and the Pits of bitumen deadly:
The Rocks of solid fire: the Ice valleys: the Plains
Of burning sand: the rivers, cataract & Lakes of Fire:
The Islands of the fiery Lakes: the Trees of Malice: Revenge:
And black Anxiety; and the Cities of the Salamandrine men:
(But whatever is visible to the Generated Man,
Is a Creation of mercy & love, from the Satanic Void.)
The land of darkness flamed but no light, & no repose:
The land of snows of trembling, & of iron hail incessant:
The land of earthquakes: and the land of woven labyrinths:
The land of snares & traps & wheels & pit-falls & dire mills:
The Voids, the Solids, & the land of clouds & regions of waters:
With their inhabitants: in the Twenty-seven Heavens beneath Beulah:
Self-righteousness conglomerating against the Divine Vision:
A Concave Earth wondrous, Chasmal, Abyssal, Incoherent!
Forming the Mundane Shell: above; beneath: on all sides surrounding
Golgonooza: Los walks round the walls night and day.
He views the City of Golgonooza & its smaller Cities:
The Looms & Mills & Prisons & Work-houses of Og & Anak:
The Amalekite: the Canaanite: the Moabite: the Egyptian:
And all that existed in the space of six thousand years:
Permanent, & not lost not lost nor vanishd, & every little act,
Word, work, & wish, that has existed, all remaining still
In those Churches ever consuming & ever building by the Spectres
Of all the inhabitants of Earth wailing to be Created:
Shadowy to those who dwell not in them, meer possibilities:
But to those who enter into them they seem the only substances
For every thing exists & not one sigh nor smile nor tear,
One hair nor particle of dust, not one can pass away.

VI

I see the Four-fold Man. The Humanity in deadly sleep
And its fallen Emanation. The Spectre & its cruel Shadow.

I see the Past, Present & Future, existing all at once
Before me; O Divine Spirit sustain me on thy wings!
That I may awake Albion from his long & cold repose.
For Bacon & Newton sheathd in dismal steel, their terrors hang
Like iron scourges over Albion, Reasonings like vast Serpents
Infold around my limbs, bruising my minute articulations
I turn my eyes to the Schools & Universities of Europe
And there behold the Loom of Locke whose Woof rages dire
Washd by the Water-wheels of Newton. black the cloth
In heavy wreathes folds over every Nation; cruel Works
Of many Wheels I view, wheel without wheel, with cogs tyrannic
Moving by compulsion each other: not as those in Eden: which
Wheel within Wheel in freedom revolve in harmony & peace.

VII

All things acted on Earth are seen in the bright Sculptures of
Los's Halls & every Age renews its powers from these Works
With every pathetic story possible to happen from Hate or
Wayward Love & every sorrow & distress is carved here
Every Affinity of Parents Marriages & Friendships are here
In all their various combinations wrought with wondrous Art
All that can happen to Man in his pilgrimage of seventy years
Such is the Divine Written Law of Horeb & Sinai:
And such the Holy Gospel of Mount Olivet & Calvary.

VIII

His Children exil'd from his breast pass to and fro before him
His birds are silent on his hills, flocks die beneath his branches
His tents are fall'n! his trumpets, and the sweet sound of his harp
Are silent on his clouded hills, that belch forth storms & fire.
His milk of Cows, & honey of Bees, & fruit of golden harvest,
Is gather'd in the scorching heat, & in the driving rain:
Where once he sat he weary walks in misery and pain:
His Giant beauty and perfection fallen into dust:
Till from within his witherd breast grown narrow with his woes:
The corn is turn'd to thistles & the apples into poison:
The birds of song to murderous crows, his joys to bitter groans!
The voices of children in his tents, to cries of helpless infants!
And self-exiled from the face of light & shine of morning,
In the dark world a narrow house! he wanders up and down,

Seeking for rest and finding none! and hidden far within,
His Eon weeping in the cold and desolated Earth.

IX

Wherefore hast thou shut me into the winter of human life
And clos'd up the sweet regions of youth and virgin innocence:
Where we live, forgetting error, not pondering on evil:
Among my lambs & brooks of water, among my warbling birds:
Where we delight in innocence before the face of the Lamb:
Going in and out before him in his love and sweet affection.

Vala replied weeping & trembling, hiding, in her veil.
When winter rends the hungry family and the snow falls:
Upon the ways of men hiding the paths of man and beast,
Then mourns the wanderer: then he repents his wanderings & eyes
The distant forest; then the slave groans in the dungeon of stone.
The captive in the mill of the stranger, sold for scanty hire.
They view their former life: they number moments over and over;
Stringing them on their remembrance as on a thread of sorrow.
Thou art my sister and my daughter! thy shame is mine also!
Ask me not of my griefs! thou knowest all my griefs.

X

Then spoke Jerusalem O Albion! my Father Albion
Why wilt thou number every little fibre of my Soul
Spreading them out before the Sun like stalks of flax to dry?
The Infant Joy is beautiful, but its anatomy
Horrible ghast & deadly! nought shalt thou find in it
But dark despair & everlasting brooding melancholy!

XI

What have I said? What have I done? O all-powerful Human Words!
You recoil back upon me in the blood of the Lamb slain in his
    Children.
Two bleeding Contraries equally true, are his Witnesses against me
We reared mighty Stones: we danced naked around them:
Thinking to bring Love into light of day, to Jerusalems shame:

Displaying our Giant limbs to all the winds of heaven! Sudden
Shame siezd us, we could not look on one-another for abhorrence: the
Blue
Of our immortal Veins & all their Hosts fled from our Limbs,
And wanderd distant in a dismal Night clouded & dark:
The Sun fled from the Britons forehead: the Moon from his mighty
loins:
Scandinavia fled with all his mountains filld with groans.
O what is Life & what is Man. O what is Death? Wherefore
Are you my Children, natives in the Grave to where I go
Or are you born to feed the hungry ravenings of Destruction
To be the sport of Accident! to waste in Wrath & Love, a weary
Life, in brooding cares & anxious labours, that prove but chaff.
O Jerusalem Jerusalem I have forsaken thy Courts
Thy Pillars of ivory & gold: thy Curtains of silk & fine
Linen: thy Pavements of precious stones: thy Walls of pearl
And gold, thy Gates of Thanksgiving thy Windows of Praise:
Thy Clouds of Blessing; thy Cherubims of Tender-mercy
Stretching their Wings sublime over the Little-ones of Albion
O Human Imagination O Divine Body I have Crucified
I have turned my back upon thee into the Wastes of Moral Law:
There Babylon is builded in the Waste, founded in Human
desolation.

O Babylon thy Watchman stands over thee in the night
Thy severe Judge all the day long proves thee O Babylon
With provings of destruction, with giving thee thy hearts desire.
But Albion is cast forth to the Potter his Children to the Builders
To build Babylon because they have forsaken Jerusalem
The Walls of Babylon are Souls of Men: her Gates the Groans
Of Nations: her Towers are the Miseries of once happy Families.
Her Streets are paved with Destruction, her Houses built with Death
Her Palaces with Hell & the Grave; her Synagogues with Torments
Of ever-hardening Despair squard & polishd with cruel skill
Yet thou wast lovely as the summer cloud upon my hills
When Jerusalem was thy hearts desire in times of youth & love.
Thy Sons came to Jerusalem with gifts, she sent them away
With blessings on their hands & on their feet, blessings of gold,
And pearl & diamond: thy Daughters sang in her Courts:
They came up to Jerusalem; they walked before Albion
In the Exchanges of London every Nation walkd

And London walkd in every Nation mutual in love & harmony
Albion coverd the whole Earth, England encompassd the Nations,
Mutual each within others bosom in Visions of Regeneration;
Jerusalem coverd the Atlantic Mountains & the Erythrean,
From bright Japan & China to Hesperia France & England.
Mount Zion lifted his head in every Nation under heaven:
And the Mount of Olives was beheld over the whole Earth:
The footsteps of the Lamb of God were there: but now no more
No more shall I behold him, he is closd in Luvahs Sepulcher.
Yet why these smitings of Luvah, the gentlest mildest Zoa?
If God was Merciful this could not be: O Lamb of God
Thou art a delusion and Jerusalem is my Sin! O my Children
I have educated you in the crucifying cruelties of Demonstration
Till you have assum'd the Providence of God & slain your Father
Dost thou appear before me who liest dead in Luvahs Sepulcher
Dost thou forgive me! thou who wast Dead & art Alive?
Look not so merciful upon me O thou Slain Lamb of God
I die! I die in thy arms tho Hope is banishd from me.

XII

I am your Rational Power O Albion & that Human Form
You call Divine, is but a Worm seventy inches long
That creeps forth in a night & is dried in the morning sun
In fortuitous concourse of memorys accumulated & lost
It plows the Earth in its own conceit, it overwhelms the Hills
Beneath its winding labyrinths, till a stone of the brook
Stops it in midst of its pride among its hills & rivers
Battersea & Chelsea mourn, London & Canterbury tremble
Their place shall not be found as the wind passes over
The ancient Cities of the Earth remove as a traveller
And shall Albions Cities remain when I pass over them
With my deluge of forgotten remembrances over the tablet
So spoke the Spectre to Albion. he is the Great Selfhood
Satan: Worshipd as God by the Mighty Ones of the Earth.

XIII

If Perceptive Organs vary: Objects of Perception seem to vary:
If the Perceptive Organs close: their Objects seem to close also:

Consider this O mortal Man! O worm of sixty winters said Los
Consider Sexual Organization & hide thee in the dust.

XIV

And many of the Eternal Ones laughed after their manner
Have you known the Judgment that is arisen among the
Zoa's of Albion? where a Man dare hardly to embrace
His own Wife, for the terrors of Chastity that they call
By the name of Morality. their Daughters govern all
In hidden deceit! they are Vegetable only fit for burning
Art & Science cannot exist but by Naked Beauty displayd
Then those in Great Eternity who contemplate on Death
Said thus. What seems to Be: Is: To those to whom
It seems to Be, & is productive of the most dreadful
Consequences to those to whom it seems to Be: even of
Torments, Despair, Eternal Death; but the Divine Mercy
Steps beyond and Redeems Man in the Body of Jesus Amen
And Length Bredth Highth again Obey the Divine Vision Hallelujah.

XV

And One stood forth from the Divine Family & said
Albion! Our wars are wars of life, & wounds of love,
With intellectual spears, & long winged arrows of thought:
Mutual in one anothers love and wrath all renewing
We live as One Man; for contracting our infinite senses
We behold multitude; or expanding: we behold as one,
As One Man all the Universal Family; and that One Man
We call Jesus the Christ: and he in us, and we in him,
Live in perfect harmony in Eden the land of life,
Giving, recieving, and forgiving each others trespasses.
He is the Good shepherd, he is the Lord and master:
He is the Shepherd of Albion, he is all in all,
In Eden: in the garden of God: and in heavenly Jerusalem.
If we have offended, forgive us, take not vengeance against us.

Thus speaking; the Divine Family follow Albion:
I see them in the Vision of God upon my pleasant valleys.
I behold London; a Human awful wonder of God!
He says: Return, Albion, return! I give myself for thee:
My Streets are my, Ideas of Imagination.
Awake Albion, awake! and let us awake up together.

My Houses are Thoughts: my Inhabitants; Affections,
The children of my thoughts, walking within my blood-vessels,
Shut from my nervous form which sleeps upon the verge of Beulah
In dreams of darkness, while my vegetating blood in veiny pipes,
Rolls dreadful thro' the Furnaces of Los, and the Mills of Satan.
For Albions sake, and for Jerusalem thy Emanation
I give myself, and these my brethren give themselves for Albion.

So spoke London, immortal Guardian! I heard in Lambeths shades:
In Felpham I heard and saw the Visions of Albion
I write in South Molton Street, what I both see and hear
In regions of Humanity, in Londons opening streets.

XVI

Then Los grew furious raging: Why stand we here trembling around
Calling on God for help; and not ourselves in whom God dwells
Stretching a hand to save the falling Man: are we not Four
Beholding Albion upon the Precipice ready to fall into Non-Entity:
Seeing these Heavens & Hells conglobing in the Void. Heavens over
Hells
Brooding in holy hypocritic lust, drinking the cries of pain
From howling victims of Law: building Heavens Twenty-seven-fold.
Swelld & bloated General Forms, repugnant to the Divine-
Humanity, who is the Only General and Universal Form
To which all Lineaments tend & seek with love & sympathy
All broad & general principles belong to benevolence
Who protects minute particulars, every one in their own identity.
But here the affectionate touch of the tongue is closd in by deadly teeth
And the soft smile of friendship & the open dawn of benevolence
Become a net & a trap, & every energy renderd cruel,
Till the existence of friendship & benevolence is denied:
The wine of the Spirit & the vineyards of the Holy-One.
Here: turn into poisonous stupor & deadly intoxication:
That they may be condemnd by Law & the Lamb of God be slain!
And the two Sources of Life in Eternity Hunting and War,
Are become the Sources of dark & bitter Death & of corroding Hell:
The open heart is shut up in integuments of frozen silence
That the spear that lights it forth may shatter the ribs & bosom
A pretence of Art, to destroy Art: a pretence of Liberty
To destroy Liberty. a pretence of Religion to destroy Religion.

XVII

Instead of Albions lovely mountains & the curtains of Jerusalem
I see a Cave, a Rock, a Tree deadly and poisonous, unimaginative:
Instead of the Mutual Forgivenesses, the Minute Particulars, I see
Pits of bitumen ever burning: artificial Riches of the Canaanite
Like Lakes of liquid lead: instead of heavenly Chapels, built
By our dear Lord: I see Worlds crusted with snows & ice;
I see a Wicker Idol woven round Jerusalems children. I see
The Canaanite, the Amalekite, the Moabite, the Egyptian:
By Demonstrations the cruel Sons of Quality & Negation.
Driven on the Void in incoherent despair into Non Entity
I see America closd apart, & Jerusalem driven in terror
Away from Albions mountains, far away from Londons spires!
I will not endure this thing! I alone withstand to death,
This outrage! Ah me! how sick & pale you all stand round me!
Ah me! pitiable ones! do you also go to deaths vale?
All you my Friends & Brothers! all you my beloved Companions!
Have you also caught the infection of Sin & stern Repentance?
I see Disease arise upon you! yet speak to me and give
Me some comfort: why do you all stand silent? I alone
Remain in permanent strength. Or is all this goodness & pity, only
That you may take the greater vengeance in your Sepulcher.

XVIII

Then the Divine Vision like a silent Sun appeard above
Albions dark rocks: setting behind the Gardens of Kensington
On Tyburns River, in clouds of blood: where was mild Zion Hills
Most ancient promontory, and in the Sun, a Human Form appeard
And thus the Voice Divine went forth upon the rocks of Albion.

XIX

And Los prayed and said. O Divine Saviour arise
Upon the Mountains of Albion as in ancient time. Behold!
The Cities of Albion seek thy face, London groans in pain
From Hill to Hill & the Thames laments along the Valleys
The little Villages of Middlesex & Surrey hunger & thirst
The Twenty-eight Cities of Albion stretch their hands to thee:
Because of the Opressors of Albion in every City & Village:
They mock at the Labourers limbs! they mock at his starvd Children.

They buy his Daughters that they may have power to sell his Sons:
They compell the Poor to live upon a crust of bread by soft mild arts:
They reduce the Man to want: then give with pomp & ceremony.
The praise of Jehovah is chaunted from lips of hunger & thirst!
Humanity knows not of Sex: wherefore are Sexes in Beulah?
In Beulah the Female lets down her beautiful Tabernacle;
Which the Male enters magnificent between her Cherubim:
And becomes One with her mingling condensing in Self-love
The Rocky Law of Condemnation & double Generation, & Death.

XX

But Los searchd in vain: closd from the minutia he walkd, difficult.
He came down from Highgate thro Hackney & Holloway towards
London
Till he came to old Stratford & thence to Stepney & the Isle
Of Leuthas Dogs, thence thro the narrows of the Rivers side
And saw every minute particular, the jewels of Albion, running down
The kennels of the streets & lanes as if they were abhorrd.
Every Universal Form, was become barren mountains of Moral
Virtue: and every Minute Particular hardend into grains of sand:
And all the tendernesses of the soul cast forth as filth & mire,
Among the winding places of deep contemplation intricate
To where the Tower of London frownd dreadful over Jerusalem:
A building of Luvah builded in Jerusalems eastern gate to be
His secluded Court: thence to Bethlehem where was builded
Dens of despair in the house of bread: enquiring in vain
Of stones and rocks he took his way, for human form was none:
And thus he spoke, looking on Albions City with many tears.

XXI

Jerusalem Jerusalem! why wilt thou turn away
Come ye O Daughters of Beulah, lament for Og & Sihon
Upon the Lakes of Ireland from Rathlin to Baltimore:
Stand ye upon the Dargle from Wicklow to Drogheda
Come & mourn over Albion the White Cliff of the Atlantic
The Mountain of Giants: all the Giants of Albion are become
Weak! witherd! darkend! & Jerusalem is cast forth from Albion.
They deny that they ever knew Jerusalem, or ever dwelt in Shiloh
The Gigantic roots & twigs of the vegetating Sons of Albion

Filld with the little-ones are consumed in the Fires of their Altars
The vegetating Cities are burned & consumed from the Earth:
And the Bodies in which all Animals & Vegetations, the Earth & Heaven
Were containd in the All Glorious Imagination are witherd & darkend;
The golden Gate of Havilah, and all the Garden of God,
Was caught up with the Sun in one day of fury and war:
The Lungs, the Heart, the Liver, shrunk away far distant from Man
And left a little slimy substance floating upon the tides.
In one night the Atlantic Continent was caught up with the Moon,
And became an Opake Globe far distant clad with moony beams.
The Visions of Eternity, by reason of narrowed perceptions,
Are become weak Visions of Time & Space, fix'd into furrows of death;
Till deep dissimulation is the only defence an honest man has left
O Polypus of Death O Spectre over Europe and Asia
Withering the Human Form by Laws of Sacrifice for Sin
By Laws of Chastity & Abhorrence I am witherd up.
Striving to Create a Heaven in which all shall be pure & holy
In their Own Selfhoods, in Natural Selfish Chastity to banish Pity
And dear Mutual Forgiveness; & to become One Great Satan
Inslavd to the most powerful Selfhood: to murder the Divine Humanity
In whose sight all are as the dust & who chargeth his Angels with folly!
Ah! weak & wide astray! Ah shut in narrow doleful form!
Creeping in reptile flesh upon the bosom of the ground!
The Eye of Man, a little narrow orb, closd up & dark,
Scarcely beholding the Great Light; conversing with the ground,
The Ear, a little shell, in small volutions shutting out
True Harmonies, & comprehending great, as very small:
The Nostrils, bent down to the earth & clos'd with senseless flesh.
That odours cannot them expand, nor joy on them exult:
The Tongue, a little moisture fills, a little food it cloys,
A little sound it utters, & its cries are faintly heard.

XXII

Silence remaind & every one resumd his Human Majesty
And many conversed on these things as they labourd at the furrow
Saying: It is better to prevent misery, than to release from misery
It is better to prevent error, than to forgive the criminal:

Labour well the Minute Particulars, attend to the Little-ones:
And those who are in misery cannot remain so long
If we do but our duty: labour well the teeming Earth.
They Plow'd in tears, the trumpets sounded before the Golden Plow
And the voices of the Living Creatures were heard in the clouds of heaven
Crying: Compell the Reasoner to Demonstrate with unhewn Demonstrations
Let the Indefinite be explored. and let every Man be Judged
By his own Works, Let all Indefinites be thrown into Demonstrations
To be pounded to dust & melted in the Furnaces of Affliction:
He who would do good to another, must do it in Minute Particulars
General Good is the plea of the scoundrel hypocrite & flatterer:
For Art & Science cannot exist but in minutely organized Particulars
And not in generalizing Demonstrations of the Rational Power.
The Infinite alone resides in Definite & Determinate Identity
Establishment of Truth depends on destruction of Falshood continually
On Circumcision: not on Virginity, O Reasoners of Albion.

XXIII

Other Daughters of Los, labouring at Looms less fine
Create the Silk-worm & the Spider & the Catterpiller
To assist in their most grievous work of pity & compassion
And others Create the wooly Lamb & the downy Fowl
To assist in the work: the Lamb bleats: the Sea-fowl cries
Men understand not the distress & the labour & sorrow
That in the Interior Worlds is carried on in fear & trembling
Weaving the shuddring fears & loves of Albions Families
Thunderous rage the Spindles of iron. & the iron Distaff
Maddens in the fury of their hands, Weaving in bitter tears
The Veil of Goats-hair & Purple & Scarlet & fine twined Linen.

XXIV

What may Man be? who can tell! But what may Woman be?
To have power over Man from Cradle to corruptible Grave.
He who is an Infant, and whose Cradle is a Manger
Knoweth the Infant sorrow: whence it came, and where it goeth:
And who weave it a Cradle of the grass that withereth away.
This World is all a Cradle for the erred wandering Phantom:

Rock'd by Year, Month, Day & Hour; and every two Moments
Between, dwells a Daughter of Beulah, to feed the Human Vegetable
Entune: Daughters of Albion. your hymning Chorus mildly!
Cord of affection thrilling extatic on the iron Reel:
To the golden Loom of Love! to the moth-labourd Woof
A Garment and Cradle weaving for the infantine Terror:
For fear; at entering the gate into our World of cruel
Lamentation: it flee back & hide in Non-Entitys dark wild
Where dwells the Spectre of Albion: destroyer of Definite Form.
The Sun shall be a Scythed Chariot of Britain: the Moon; a Ship
In the British Ocean! Created by Los's Hammer; measured out
Into Days & Nights & Years & Months. to travel with my feet
Over these desolate rocks of Albion: O daughters of despair!
Rock the Cradle, and in mild melodies tell me where found
What you have enwoven with so much tears & care? so much
Tender artifice: to laugh: to weep: to learn: to know;
Remember! recollect! what dark befel in wintry days.

XXV

In Great Eternity, every particular Form gives forth or Emanates
Its own peculiar Light, & the Form is the Divine Vision
And the Light is his Garment This is Jerusalem in every Man
A Tent & Tabernacle of Mutual Forgiveness Male & Female
Clothings.
And Jerusalem is called Liberty among the Children of Albion.

XXVI

Behold: in the Visions of Elohim Jehovah. behold Joseph & Mary
And be comforted O Jerusalem in the Visions of Jehovah Elohim
She looked & saw Joseph the Carpenter in Nazareth & Mary
His espoused Wife. And Mary said, If thou put me away from thee
Dost thou not murder me? Joseph spoke in anger & fury. Should I
Marry a Harlot & an Adulteress? Mary answerd, Art thou more pure
Than thy Maker who forgiveth Sins & calls again Her that is Lost
Tho She hates. he calls her again in love. I love my dear Joseph
But he driveth me away from his presence. yet I hear the voice of God
In the voice of my Husband. tho he is angry for a moment, he will not
Utterly cast me away. if I were pure, never could I taste the sweets
Of the Forgiveness of Sins! if I were holy! I never could behold the tears
Of love! of him who loves me in the midst of his anger in furnace of fire.

Ah my Mary: said Joseph: weeping over & embracing her closely in
His arms: Doth he forgive Jerusalem & not exact Purity from her who is
Polluted. I heard his voice in my sleep & his Angel in my dream:
Saying, Doth Jehovah Forgive a Debt only on condition that it shall
Be Payed? Doth he Forgive Pollution only on conditions of Purity
That Debt is not Forgiven! That Pollution is not Forgiven
Such is the Forgiveness of the Gods, the Moral Virtues of the
Heathen, whose tender Mercies are Cruelty. But Jehovahs Salvation
Is without Money & without Price, in the Continual Forgiveness of Sins
In the Perpetual Mutual Sacrifice in Great Eternity! for behold!
There is none that liveth & Sinneth not! And this is the Covenant
Of Jehovah: If you Forgive one-another, so shall Jehovah Forgive You:
That He Himself may Dwell among You. Fear not then to take
To thee Mary thy Wife, for she is with Child by the Holy Ghost.

Then Mary burst forth into a Song! she flowed like a River of
Many Streams in the arms of Joseph & gave forth her tears of joy
Like many waters, and Emanating into gardens & palaces upon
Euphrates & to forests & floods & animals wild & tame from
Gihon to Hiddekel, & to corn fields & villages & inhabitants
Upon Pison & Arnon & Jordan. And I heard the voice among
The Reapers Saying, Am I Jerusalem the lost Adulteress? or am I
Babylon come up to Jerusalem? And another voice answerd Saying
Does the voice of my Lord call me again? am I pure thro his Mercy
And Pity. Am I become lovely as a Virgin in his sight who am
Indeed a Harlot drunken with the Sacrifice of Idols does he
Call her pure as he did in the days of her Infancy when She
Was cast out to the loathing of her person. The Chaldean took
Me from my Cradle. The Amalekite stole me away upon his Camels
Before I had ever beheld with love the Face of Jehovah; or known
That there was a God of Mercy: O Mercy O Divine Humanity!
O Forgiveness & Pity & Compassion! If I were Pure I should never
Have Known Thee; If I were Unpolluted I should never have
Glorified thy Holiness, or rejoiced in thy great Salvation.

Mary leaned her side against Jerusalem, Jerusalem recieved
The Infant into her hands in the Visions of Jehovah. Times passed on
Jerusalem fainted over the Cross & Sepulcher She heard the voice
Wilt thou make Rome thy Patriarch Druid & the Kings of Europe his

Horsemen? Man in the Resurrection changes his Sexual Garments at will
Every Harlot was once a Virgin: every Criminal an Infant Love!

XXVII

Then left the Sons of Urizen the plow & harrow, the loom
The hammer & the chisel, & the rule & compasses; from London fleeing
They forg'd the sword on Cheviot, the chariot of war & the battle-ax,
The trumpet fitted to mortal battle, & the flute of summer in Annandale
And all the Arts of Life. they changd into the Arts of Death in Albion.
The hour-glass contemnd because its simple workmanship.
Was like the workmanship of the plowman, & the water wheel,
That raises water into cisterns: broken & burnd with fire:
Because its workmanship. was like the workmanship of the shepherd.
And in their stead, intricate wheels invented, wheel without wheel:
To perplex youth in their outgoings, & to bind to labours in Albion
Of day & night the myriads of eternity that they may grind
And polish brass & iron hour after hour laborious task!
Kept ignorant of its use, that they might spend the days of wisdom
In sorrowful drudgery, to obtain a scanty pittance of bread:
In ignorance to view a small portion & think that All,
And call it Demonstration: blind to all the simple rules of life.
Now: now the battle rages round thy tender limbs O Vala
Now smile among thy bitter tears: now put on all thy beauty
Is not the wound of the sword sweet! & the broken bone delightful?
Wilt thou now smile among the scythes when the wounded groan in the field
We were carried away in thousands from London; & in tens
Of thousands from Westminster & Marybone in ships closd up.

XXVIII

Compelld to leave the plow to the ox, to snuff up the winds of desolation
To trample the corn fields in boastful neighings: this is no gentle harp
This is no warbling brook, nor shadow of a mirtle tree:
But blood and wounds and dismal cries, and shadows of the oak:
And hearts laid open to the light, by the broad grizly sword:

And bowels hid in hammerd steel rip'd quivering on the ground.
Call forth thy smiles of soft deceit: call forth thy cloudy tears:
We hear thy sighs in trumpets shrill when morn shall blood renew.

XXIX

They turn, contorted: their iron necks bend unwilling towards
Luvah: their lips tremble: their muscular fibres are crampd & smitten
They become like what they behold! Yet immense in strength &
power,
In awful pomp & gold, in all the precious unhewn stones of Eden
They build a stupendous Building on the Plain of Salisbury; with
chains
Of rocks round London Stone: of Reasonings: of unhewn
Demonstrations
In labyrinthine arches. (Mighty Urizen the Architect.) thro which
The Heavens might revolve & Eternity be bound in their chain.
Labour unparallelld! a wondrous rocky World of cruel destiny
Rocks piled on rocks reaching the stars: stretching from pole to pole.
The Building is Natural Religion & its Altars Natural Morality
A building of eternal death: whose proportions are eternal despair.

XXX

I am drunk with unsatiated love
I must rush again to War: for the Virgin has frownd & refusd
Sometimes I curse & sometimes bless thy fascinating beauty
Once Man was occupied in intellectual pleasures & energies
But now my soul is harrowd with grief & fear & love & desire
And now I hate & now I love & Intellect is no more:
There is no time for any thing but the torments of love & desire
The Feminine & Masculine Shadows soft, mild & ever varying
In beauty: are Shadows now no more, but Rocks in Horeb.

XXXI

Hence the Infernal Veil grows in the disobedient Female:
Which Jesus rends & the whole Druid Law removes away
From the Inner Sanctuary: a False Holiness hid within the Center,
For the Sanctuary of Eden. is in the Camp: in the Outline,
In the Circumference: & every Minute Particular is Holy:

Embraces are Cominglings: from the Head even to the Feet;
And not a pompous High Priest entering by a Secret Place.

XXXII

The Spectre is the Reasoning Power in Man; & when separated
From Imagination, and closing itself as in steel, in a Ratio
Of the Things of Memory. It thence frames Laws & Moralities
To destroy Imagination! the Divine Body, by Martyrdoms & Wars
Teach me O Holy Spirit the Testimony of Jesus! let me
Comprehend wonderous things out of the Divine Law
I behold Babylon in the opening Street of London, I behold
Jerusalem in ruins wandering about from house to house
This I behold the shudderings of death attend my steps
I walk up and down in Six Thousand Years: their Events are present
before me.

XXXIII

Highgates heights & Hampsteads, to Poplar Hackney & Bow:
To Islington & Paddington & the Brook of Albions River
We builded Jerusalem as a City & a Temple; from Lambeth
We began our Foundations; lovely Lambeth! O lovely Hills
Of Camberwell, we shall behold you no more in glory & pride
For Jerusalem lies in ruins & the Furnaces of Los are builded there
You are now shrunk up to a narrow Rock in the midst of the Sea
But here we build Babylon on Euphrates, compelld to build
And to inhabit, our Little-ones to clothe in armour of the gold
Of Jerusalems Cherubims & to forge them swords of her Altars
I see London blind & age-bent begging thro the Streets
Of Babylon, led by a child. his tears run down his beard
The voice of Wandering Reuben ecchoes from street to street
In all the Cities of the Nations Paris Madrid Amsterdam
The Corner of Broad Street weeps; Poland Street languishes
To Great Queen Street & Lincolns Inn, all is distress & woe.

XXXIV

It is easier to forgive an Enemy than to forgive a Friend:
The man who permits you to injure him, deserves your vengeance:
He also will recieve it; go Spectre! obey my most secret desire:
Which thou knowest without my speaking: Go to these Fiends of
Righteousness

Tell them to obey their Humanities, & not pretend Holiness;
When they are murderers: as far as my Hammer & Anvil permit
Go, tell them that the Worship of God, is honouring his gifts
In other men: & loving the greatest men best, each according
To his Genius: which is the Holy Ghost in Man; there is no other
God, than that God who is the intellectual fountain of Humanity;
He who envies or calumniates: which is murder & cruelty,
Murders the Holy-one: Go tell them this & overthrow their cup,
Their bread, their altar-table, their incense & their oath:
Their marriage & their baptism, their burial & consecration:
I have tried to make friends by corporeal gifts but have only
Made enemies: I never made friends but by spiritual gifts;
By severe contentions of friendship & the burning fire of thought.
He who would see the Divinity must see him in his Children
One first, in friendship & love; then a Divine Family, & in the midst
Jesus will appear; so he who wishes to see a Vision; a perfect Whole
Must see it in its Minute Particulars; Organized & not as thou
O Fiend of Righteousness pretendest; thine is a Disorganized
And snowy cloud: brooder of tempests & destructive War
You smile with pomp & rigor: you talk of benevolence & virtue!
I act with benevolence & virtue & get murdered time after time:
You accumulate Particulars, & murder by analyzing, that you
May take the aggregate; & you call the aggregate Moral law:
And you call that Swelld & bloated Form; a Minute Particular.
But General Forms have their vitality in Particulars: & every
Particular is a Man; a Divine Member of the Divine Jesus.

XXXV

Deny a conscience in Man & the Communion of Saints & Angels
Contemning the Divine Vision & Fruition, Worshiping the Deus
Of the Heathen, The God of This World, & the Goddess Nature
Mystery Babylon the Great, The Druid Dragon & hidden Harlot
Is it not that Signal of the Morning which was told us in the Beginning.

XXXVI

Time was Finished! The Breath Divine Breathed over Albion
Beneath the Furnaces & starry Wheels and in the Immortal Tomb
And England who is Brittannia awoke from Death on Albions bosom
She awoke pale & cold she fainted seven times on the Body of Albion
O pitious Sleep O pitious Dream! O God O God awake I have slain

In Dreams of Chastity & Moral Law I have Murdered Albion! Ah!
In Stone-henge & on London Stone & in the Oak Groves of Malden
I have Slain him in my Sleep with the Knife of the Druid O England
O all ye Nations of the Earth behold ye the Jealous Wife
The Eagle & the Wolf & Monkey & Owl & the King & Priest were
there
Her voice pierc'd Albions clay cold ear. he moved upon the Rock
The Breath Divine went forth upon the morning hills, Albion mov'd
Upon the Rock, he opend his eyelids in pain; in pain he mov'd
His stony members, he saw England. Ah! shall the Dead live again?

XXXVII

Then Jesus appeared standing by Albion as the Good Shepherd
By the lost Sheep that he hath found & Albion knew that it
Was the Lord the Universal Humanity, & Albion saw his Form
A Man. & they conversed as Man with Man, in Ages of Eternity
And the Divine Appearance was the likeness & similitude of Los.

XXXVIII

Jesus replied Fear not Albion unless I die thou canst not live
But if I die I shall arise again & thou with me
This is Friendship & Brotherhood without it Man Is Not.

XXXIX

Albion replyd. Cannot Man exist without Mysterious
Offering of Self for Another, is this Friendship & Brotherhood
I see thee in the likeness & similitude of Los my Friend
Jesus said. Wouldest thou love one who never died
For thee or ever die for one who had not died for thee
And if God dieth not for Man & giveth not himself
Eternally for Man Man could not exist. for Man is Love:
As God is Love: every kindness to another is a little Death
In the Divine Image nor can Man exist but by Brotherhood.

XL

Awake! Awake Jerusalem! O lovely Emanation of Albion
Awake and overspread all Nations as in Ancient Time
For lo! the Night of Death is past and the Eternal Day
Appears upon our Hills: Awake Jerusalem, and come away.

XLI

And they conversed together in Visionary forms dramatic which
bright
Redounded from their Tongues in thunderous majesty, in Visions
In new Expanses, creating exemplars of Memory and of Intellect
Creating Space, Creating Time according to the wonders Divine
Of Human Imagination, throughout all the Three Regions immense
Of Childhood, Manhood & Old Age & the all tremendous
unfathomable Non Ens
Of Death was seen in regenerations terrific or complacent varying
According to the subject of discourse & every Word & Every
Character
Was Human according to the Expansion or Contraction, the
Translucence or
Opakeness of Nervous fibres such was the variation of Time & Space
Which vary according as the Organs of Perception vary & they walked
To & fro in Eternity as One Man reflecting each in each & clearly seen
And seeing: according to fitness & order. And I heard Jehovah speak
Terrific from his Holy Place & saw the Words of the Mutual Covenant
Divine
On Chariots of gold & jewels with Living Creatures starry & flaming
With every Colour, Lion, Tyger, Horse, Elephant, Eagle, Dove, Fly,
Worm,
And the all wondrous Serpent clothed in gems & rich array Humanize
In the Forgiveness of Sins according to the Covenant of Jehovah. They
Cry
Where is the Covenant of Priam, the Moral Virtues of the Heathen
Where is the Tree of Good & Evil that rooted beneath the cruel heel
Of Albions Spectre the Patriarch Druid! where are all his Human
Sacrifices
For Sin in War & in the Druid Temples of the Accuser of Sin: beneath
The Oak Groves of Albion that coverd the whole Earth beneath his
Spectre
Where are the Kingdoms of the World & all their glory that grew on
Desolation
The Fruit of Albions Poverty Tree when the Triple Headed
Gog-Magog Giant
Of Albion Taxed the Nations into Desolation & then gave the
Spectrous Oath

Such is the Cry from all the Earth from the Living Creatures of the
Earth

And from the great City of Golgonooza in the Shadowy Generation
And from the Thirty-two Nations of the Earth among the Living
Creatures
All Human Forms identified even Tree Metal Earth & Stone. all
Human Forms identified, living going forth & returning wearied
Into the Planetary lives of Years Months Days & Hours reposing
And then Awaking into his Bosom in the Life of Immortality.
And I heard the Name of their Emanations they are named Jerusalem.

Verses from *The Gates of Paradise*

I

Mutual Forgiveness of each Vice
Such are the Gates of Paradise
Against the Accusers chief desire
Who walkd among the Stones of Fire
Jehovahs Finger Wrote the Law
Then Wept! then rose in Zeal & Awe
And the Dead Corpse from Sinais heat
Buried beneath his Mercy Seat
O Christians Christians! tell me Why
You rear it on your Altars high?

II

To The Accuser who is The God of This World

Truly My Satan thou art but a Dunce
And dost not know the Garment from the Man
Every Harlot was a Virgin once
Nor canst thou ever change Kate into Nan

Tho thou art Worshipd by the Names Divine
Of Jesus & Jehovah: thou art still
The Son of Morn in weary Nights decline
The lost Travellers Dream under the Hill.

Laments from *The Four Zoas*

I

Enion said – Thy fear has made me tremble thy terrors have
surrounded me
All Love is lost Terror succeeds & Hatred instead of Love
And stern demands of Right & Duty instead of Liberty.
Once thou wast to Me the loveliest son of heaven – But now
Why art thou Terrible and yet I love thee in thy terror till
I am almost Extinct & soon shall be a Shadow in Oblivion
Unless some way can be found that I may look upon thee & live
Hide me some Shadowy semblance. secret whispring in my Ear
In secret of soft wings. in mazes of delusive beauty
I have lookd into the secret soul of him I lovd
And in the Dark recesses found Sin & cannot return

Trembling & pale sat Tharmas weeping in his clouds
Why wilt thou Examine every little fibre of my soul
Spreading them out before the Sun like Stalks of flax to dry
The infant joy is beautiful but its anatomy
Horrible Ghast & Deadly nought shalt thou find in it
But Death Despair & Everlasting brooding Melancholy
Thou wilt go mad with horror if thou dost Examine thus
Every moment of my secret hours Yea I know
That I have sinnd & that my Emanations are become harlots
I am already distracted at their deeds & if I look
Upon them more Despair will bring self murder on my soul
O Enion thou art thyself a root growing in hell
Tho thus heavenly beautiful to draw me to destruction
Sometimes I think thou art a flower expanding
Sometimes I think thou art fruit breaking from its bud
In dreadful dolor & pain & I am like an atom
A Nothing left in darkness yet I am an identity
I wish & feel & weep & groan Ah terrible terrible.

II

And Tharmas calld to the Dark Spectre who upon the Shores
With dislocated Limbs had falln. The Spectre rose in pain
A Shadow blue obscure & dismal. like a statue of lead
Bent by its fall from a high tower the dolorous shadow rose.

III

And he said Wherefore do I feel such love & pity
Ah Enion Ah Enion Ah lovely lovely Enion
How is this All my hope is gone for ever fled
Like a famishd Eagle Eyeless raging in the vast expanse
Incessant tears are now my food. incessant rage & tears
Deathless for ever now I wander seeking oblivion
In torrents of despair in vain. for if I plunge beneath
Stifling I live. If dashd in pieces from a rocky height
I reunite in endless torment. would I had never risen
From deaths cold sleep beneath the bottom of the raging Ocean
And cannot those who once have lovd. ever forget their Love?
Are love & rage the same passion? they are the same in me
Are those who love. like those who died. risen again from death
Immortal. in immortal torment. never to be deliverd
Is it not possible that one risen again from Death
Can die! When dark despair comes over can I not
Flow down into the sea & slumber in oblivion. Ah Enion!

IV

I am made to sow the thistle for wheat; the nettle for a nourishing
    dainty
I have planted a false oath in the earth, it has brought forth a poison
    tree
I have chosen the serpent for a councellor & the dog
For a schoolmaster to my children
I have blotted out from light & living the dove & nightingale
And I have caused the earth worm to beg from door to door
I have taught the thief a secret path into the house of the just
I have taught pale artifice to spread his nets upon the morning
My heavens are brass my earth is iron my moon a clod of clay
My sun a pestilence burning at noon & a vapour of death in night

What is the price of Experience do men buy it for a song
Or wisdom for a dance in the street? No it is bought with the price
Of all that a man hath his house his wife his children
Wisdom is sold in the desolate market where none come to buy
And in the witherd field where the farmer plows for bread in vain

It is an easy thing to triumph in the summers sun
And in the vintage & to sing on the waggon loaded with corn

It is an easy thing to talk of patience to the afflicted
To speak the laws of prudence to the houseless wanderer
To listen to the hungry ravens cry in wintry season
When the red blood is filld with wine & with the marrow of lambs
It is an easy thing to laugh at wrathful elements
To hear the dog howl at the wintry door, the ox in the slaughter house
moan
To see a god on every wind & a blessing on every blast
To hear sounds of love in the thunder storm that destroys our enemies
house
To rejoice in the blight that covers his field, & the sickness that cuts off
his children
While our olive & vine sing & laugh round our door & our children
bring fruits & flowers
Then the groan & the dolor are quite forgotten & the slave grinding at
the mill
And the captive in chains & the poor in the prison, & the soldier in the
field
When the shatterd bone hath laid him groaning among the happier
dead
It is an easy thing to rejoice in the tents of prosperity
Thus could I sing & thus rejoice, but it is not so with me!

V

The King of Light beheld her mourning among the Brick kilns
compelld
To labour night & day among the fires, her lamenting voice
Is heard when silent night returns & the labourers take their rest

O Lord wilt thou not look upon our sore afflictions
Among these flames incessant labouring, our hard masters laugh
At all our sorrow. We are made to turn the wheel for water
To carry the heavy basket on our scorched shoulders, to sift
The sand & ashes, & to mix the clay with tears & repentance
I see not Luvah as of old I only see his feet
Like pillars of fire travelling thro darkness & non entity
The times are now returnd upon us, we have given ourselves
To scorn and now are scorned by the slaves of our enemies
Our beauty is coverd over with clay & ashes, & our backs
Furrowd with whips, & our flesh bruised with the heavy basket
Forgive us O thou piteous one whom we have offended, forgive
The weak remaining shadow of Vala that returns in sorrow to thee.

VI

Why does the Raven cry aloud and no eye pities her?
Why fall the Sparrow & the Robin in the foodless winter?
Faint! shivering they sit on leafless bush, or frozen stone

Wearied with seeking food across the snowy waste; the little
Heart, cold; and the little tongue consum'd, that once in thoughtless joy
Gave songs of gratitude to waving corn fields round their nest

Why howl the Lion & the Wolf? why do they roam abroad?
Deluded by summers heat they sport in enormous love
And cast their young out to the hungry wilds & sandy desarts

Why is the Sheep given to the knife? the Lamb plays in the Sun
He starts! he hears the foot of Man! he says, Take thou my wool
But spare my life, but he knows not that winter cometh fast.

The Spider sits in his labourd Web, eager watching for the Fly
Presently comes a famishd Bird & takes away the Spider
His Web is left all desolate, that his little anxious heart
So careful wove; & spread it out with sighs and weariness

VII

My fountains once the haunt of Swans now breed the scaly tortoise
The houses of my harpers are become a haunt of crows
The gardens of wisdom are become a field of horrid graves
And on the bones I drop my tears & water them in vain
Once how I walked from my palace in gardens of delight
The sons of wisdom stood around the harpers followd with harps
Nine virgins clothd in light composd the song to their immortal voices
And at my banquets of new wine my head was crownd with joy
Then in my ivory pavilions I slumberd in the noon
And walked in the silent night among sweet smelling flowers
Till on my silver bed I slept & sweet dreams round me hoverd
But now my land is darkend & my wise men are departed
My songs are turned to cries of Lamentation
Heard on my Mountains & deep sighs under my palace roofs
Because the Steeds of Urizen once swifter than the light
Were kept back from my Lord & from his chariot of mercies

O did I keep the horses of the day in silver pastures
O I refusd the Lord of day the horses of his prince
O did I close my treasuries with roofs of solid stone
And darken all my Palace walls with envyings & hate
O Fool to think that I could hide from his all piercing eyes
The gold & silver & costly stones his holy workmanship
O Fool could I forget the light that filled my bright spheres
Was a reflection of his face who calld me from the deep
I well remember for I heard the mild & holy voice
Saying O light spring up & shine & I sprang up from the deep
He gave to me a silver scepter & crownd me with a golden crown
& said Go forth & guide my Son who wanders on the ocean
I went not forth. I hid myself in black clouds of my wrath
I calld the stars around my feet in the night of councils dark
The stars threw down their spears & fled naked away
We fell.

VIII

Urizen wept in the dark deep anxious his Scaly form
To reassume the human & he wept in the dark deep
Saying O that I had never drank the wine nor eat the bread
Of dark mortality nor cast my view into futurity nor turnd
My back darkning the present clouding with a cloud
And building arches high & cities turrets & towers & domes
Whose smoke destroyd the pleasant gardens & whose running
Kennels
Chokd the bright rivers burdning with my Ships the angry deep
Thro Chaos seeking for delight & in spaces remote
Seeking the Eternal which is always present to the wise
Seeking for pleasure which unsought falls round the infants path
And on the fleeces of mild flocks who neither care nor labour.

IX

Thou knowest that the Spectre is in Every Man insane brutish
Deformd that I am thus a ravening devouring lust continually
Craving & devouring but my Eyes are always upon thee O lovely
Delusion & I cannot crave for any thing but thee not so
The spectres of the Dead for I am as the Spectre of the Living
For till these terrors planted round the Gates of Eternal life
Are driven away & annihilated we never can repass the Gates.

X

Compell the poor to live upon a Crust of bread by soft mild arts
Smile when they frown frown when they smile & when a man looks
    pale
With labour & abstinence say he looks healthy & happy
And when his children sicken let them die there are enough
Born even too many & our Earth will be overrun
Without these arts If you would make the poor live with temper
With pomp give every crust of bread you give with gracious cunning
Magnify small gifts reduce the man to want a gift & then give with
    pomp
Say he smiles if you hear him sigh If pale say he is ruddy
Preach temperance say he is overgorgd & drowns his wit
In strong drink tho you know that bread & water are all
He can afford Flatter his wife pity his children till we can
Reduce all to our will as spaniels are taught with art.

XI

I wakened Enion in the Morning & she turnd away
Among the apple trees & all the gardens of delight
Swam like a dream before my eyes I went to seek the steps
Of Enion in the gardens & the shadows compassd me
And closd me in a watry world of woe where Enion stood
Trembling before me like a shadow like a mist like air
And she is gone & here alone I war with darkness & death
I hear thy voice but not thy form see. thou & all delight
And life appear & vanish mocking me with shadows of false hope.

XII

On this rock lay the faded head of the Eternal Man
Enwrapped round with weeds of death pale cold in sorrow & woe
He lifts the blue lamps of his Eyes & cries with heavenly voice
Bowing his head over the consuming Universe he cried
O weakness & O weariness O war within my members
My sons exiled from my breast pass to & fro before me
My birds are silent on my hills flocks die beneath my branches
My tents are fallen my trumpets & the sweet sounds of my harp
Is silent on my clouded hills that belch forth storms & fires
My milk of cows & honey of bees & fruit of golden harvest

Are gatherd in the scorching heat & in the driving rain
My robe is turned to confusion & my bright gold to stones
Where once I sat I weary walk in misery & pain
For from within my witherd breast grown narrow with my woes
The Corn is turnd to thistles & the apples into poison
The birds of song to murderous crows My joys to bitter groans
The voices of children in my tents to cries of helpless infants
And all exiled from the face of light & shine of morning
In this dark world a narrow house I wander up & down
I hear Mystery howling in these flames of Consummation
When shall the Man of future times become as in days of old
O weary life why sit I here & give up all my powers
To indolence to the night of death when indolence & mourning
Sit hovring over my dark threshold. tho I arise look out
And scorn the war within my members yet my heart is weak
And my head faint Yet will I look again unto the morning
Whence is this sound of rage of Men drinking each others blood
Drunk with the smoking gore & red but not with nourishing wine

The Eternal Man sat on the Rocks & cried with awful voice.

Episodes from *The Four Zoas*

I

But when fourteen summers & winters had revolved over
Their solemn habitation Los beheld the ruddy boy
Embracing his bright mother & beheld malignant fires
In his young eyes discerning plain that Orc plotted his death
Grief rose upon his ruddy brows. a tightening girdle grew
Around his bosom like a bloody cord. in secret sobs
He burst it, but next morn another girdle succeeds
Around his bosom. Every day he viewd the fiery youth
With silent fear & his immortal cheeks grew deadly pale
Till many a morn & many a night passd over in dire woe
Forming a girdle in the day & bursting it at night
The girdle was formd by day by night was burst in twain
Falling down on the rock an iron chain link by link lockd

Enitharmon beheld the bloody chain of nights & days
Depending from the bosom of Los & how with grinding pain
He went each morning to his labours with the spectre dark
Calld it the chain of Jealousy. Now Los began to speak
His woes aloud to Enitharmon. since he could not hide
His uncouth plague. He siezd the boy in his immortal hands
While Enitharmon followd him weeping in dismal woe
Up to the iron mountains top & there the Jealous chain
Fell from his bosom on the mountain. The Spectre dark
Held the fierce boy Los naild him down binding around his limbs
The accursed chain O how bright Enitharmon howld & cried
Over her son. Obdurate Los bound down her loved Joy
The hammer of Urthona smote the rivets in terror. of brass
Tenfold. the Demons rage flamd tenfold forth rending
Roaring redounding. Loud Loud Louder & Louder & fird
The darkness warring with the waves of Tharmas & Snows of Urizen
Crackling the flames went up with fury from the immortal demon
Surrounded with flames the Demon grew loud howling in his fires
Los folded Enitharmon in a cold white cloud in fear
Then led her down into the deeps & into his labyrinth
Giving the Spectre sternest charge over the howling fiend
Concentered into Love of Parent Storgous Appetite Craving

His limbs bound down mock at his chains for over them a flame

Of circling fire unceasing plays to feed them with life & bring
The virtues of the Eternal worlds ten thousand thousand spirits
Of life lament around the Demon going forth & returning
At his enormous call they flee into the heavens of heavens
And back return with wine & food. Or dive into the deeps
To bring the thrilling joys of sense to quell his ceaseless rage
His eyes the lights of his large soul contract or else expand
Contracted they behold the secrets of the infinite mountains
The veins of gold & silver & the hidden things of Vala
Whatever grows from its pure bud or breathes a fragrant soul
Expanded they behold the terrors of the Sun & Moon
The Elemental Planets & the orbs of eccentric fire
His nostrils breathe a fiery flame. his locks are like the forests
Of wild beasts there the lion glares the tyger & wolf howl there
And there the Eagle hides her young in cliffs & precipices
His bosom is like starry heaven expanded all the stars
Sing round. there waves the harvest & the vintage rejoices. the Springs
Flow into rivers of delight. there the spontaneous flowers
Drink laugh & sing. the grasshopper the Emmet & the Fly
The golden Moth builds there a house & spreads her silken bed
His loins inwove with silken fires are like a furnace fierce
As the strong Bull in summer time when bees sing round the heath
Where the herds low after the shadow & after the water spring
The numrous flocks cover the mountain & shine along the valley
His knees are rocks of adamant & rubie & emerald
Spirits of strength in Palaces rejoice in golden armour
Armed with spear & shield they drink and rejoice over the slain
Such is the Demon such his terror in the nether deep

But when returnd to Golgonooza Los & Enitharmon
Felt all the sorrow Parents feel. they wept toward one another
And Los repented that he had chaind Orc upon the mountain
And Enitharmons tears prevaild parental love returnd
Tho terrible his dread of that infernal chain They rose
At midnight hasting to their much beloved care
Nine days they traveld thro the Gloom of Entuthon Benithon
Los taking Enitharmon by the hand led her along
The dismal vales & up to the iron mountains top where Orc
Howld in the furious wind he thought to give to Enitharmon
Her son in tenfold joy & to compensate for her tears
Even if his own death resulted so much pity him paind

But when they came to the dark rock & to the spectrous cave
Lo the young limbs had strucken root into the rock & strong
Fibres had from the Chain of Jealousy inwove themselves
In a swift vegetation round the rock & round the Cave
And over the immortal limbs of the terrible fiery boy
In vain they strove now to unchain. In vain with bitter tears
To melt the chain of Jealousy. not Enitharmons death
Nor the Consummation of Los could ever melt the chain
Nor unroot the infernal fibres from their rocky bed
Nor all Urthonas strength nor all the power of Luvahs Bulls
Tho they each morning drag the unwilling Sun out of the deep
Could uproot the infernal chain. for it had taken root
Into the iron rock & grew a chain beneath the Earth
Even to the Center wrapping round the Center & the limbs
Of Orc entering with fibres. became one with him a living Chain
Sustained by the Demons life. Despair & Terror & Woe & Rage
Inwrap the Parents in cold clouds as they bend howling over
The terrible boy till fainting by his side the Parents fell
Not long they lay Urthonas spectre found herbs of the pit
Rubbing their temples he reviv'd them. all their lamentations
I write not here but all their after life was lamentation.

II

But Urizen silent descended to the Caves of Orc & saw
A Cavernd Universe of flaming fire the horses of Urizen
Here bound to fiery mangers furious dash their golden hoofs
Striking fierce sparkles from their brazen fetters. fierce his loins
Howl in the burning dens his tygers roam in the redounding smoke
In forests of affliction. the adamantine scales of justice
Consuming in the raging lamps of mercy pourd in rivers
The holy oil rages thro all the cavernd rocks fierce flames
Dance on the rivers & the rocks howling & drunk with fury
The plow of ages & the golden harrow wade thro fields
Of goary blood the immortal seed is nourishd for the slaughter
The bulls of Luvah breathing fire bellow on burning pastures
Round howling Orc whose awful limbs cast forth red smoke & fire
That Urizen approachd not near but took his seat on a rock
And rangd his books around him brooding Envious over Orc.

III

The time of Prophecy is now revolvd & all
This Universal Ornament is mine & in my hands
The ends of heaven like a Garment will I fold them round me
Consuming what must be consumd then in power & majesty
I will walk forth thro those wide fields of endless Eternity
A God & not a Man a Conqueror in triumphant glory
And all the Sons of Everlasting shall bow down at my feet

First Trades & Commerce ships & armed vessels he builded laborious
To swim the deep & on the Land children are sold to trades
Of dire necessity still laboring day & night till all
Their life extinct they took the spectre form in dark despair
And slaves in myriads in ship loads burden the hoarse sounding deep
Rattling with clanking chains the Universal Empire groans
And he commanded his Sons found a Center in the Deep
And Urizen laid the first stone & all his myriads
Builded a temple in the image of the human heart
And in the inner part of the Temple wondrous workmanship
They formd the Secret place reversing all the order of delight
That whosoever enterd into the temple might not behold
The hidden wonders allegoric of the Generations
Of secret lust when hid in chambers dark the nightly harlot
Plays in Disguise in whisperd hymn & mumbling prayer The priests
He ordaind & Priestesses clothd in disguises bestial
Inspiring secrecy & lamps they bore intoxicating fumes
Roll round the Temple & they took the Sun that glowd oer Los
And with immense machines down rolling. the terrific orb
Compell'd. The Sun reddning like a fierce lion in his chains
Descended to the sound of instruments that drownd the noise
Of the hoarse wheels & the terrific howlings of wild beasts
That dragd the wheels of the Suns chariot & they put the Sun
Into the temple of Urizen to give light to the Abyss
To light the War by day to hide his secret beams by night
For he divided day & night in different orderd portions
The day for war the night for secret religion in his temple.

IV

Thus was the Lamb of God condemnd to Death
They naild him upon the tree of Mystery weeping over him
And then mocking & then worshipping calling him Lord & King

Sometimes as twelve daughters lovely & sometimes as five
They stood in beaming beauty & sometimes as one even Rahab
Who is Mystery Babylon the Great the Mother of Harlots
Jerusalem saw the Body dead upon the Cross She fled away
Saying Is this Eternal Death Where shall I hide from Death
Pity me Los pity me Urizen & let us build
A Sepulcher & worship Death in fear while yet we live
Death! God of All from whom we rise to whom we all return
And Let all Nations of the Earth worship at the Sepulcher
With Gifts & Spices with lamps rich embossd jewels & gold

Los took the Body from the Cross Jerusalem weeping over
They bore it to the Sepulcher which Los had hewn in the rock
Of Eternity for himself he hewd it despairing of Life Eternal.

V

And all the time in Caverns shut, the golden Looms erected
First spun, then wove the Atmospheres, there the Spider & Worm
Plied the wingd shuttle piping shrill thro' all the list'ning threads
Beneath the Caverns roll the weights of lead & spindles of iron
The enormous warp & woof rage direful in the affrighted deep
While far into the vast unknown, the strong wing'd Eagles bend
Their venturous flight, in Human forms distinct; thro darkness deep
They bear the woven draperies; on golden hooks they hang abroad
The universal curtains & spread out from Sun to Sun
The vehicles of light, they separate the furious particles
Into mild currents as the water mingles with the wine.

While thus the Spirits of strongest wing enlighten the dark deep
The threads are spun & the cords twisted & drawn out; then the weak
Begin their work; & many a net is netted; many a net
Spread & many a Spirit caught, innumerable the nets
Innumerable the gins & traps; & many a soothing flute
Is form'd & many a corded lyre, outspread over the immense
In cruel delight they trap the listeners, & in cruel delight
Bind them, condensing the strong energies into little compass
Some became seed of every plant that shall be planted; some
The bulbous roots, thrown up together into barns & garners

Then rose the Builders; First the Architect divine his plan
Unfolds, The wondrous scaffold reard all round the infinite
Quadrangular the building rose the heavens squared by a line.

Trigon & cubes divide the elements in finite bonds
Multitudes without number work incessant: the hewn stone
Is placd in beds of mortar mingled with the ashes of Vala
Severe the labour, female slaves the mortar trod oppressed
Twelve halls after the names of his twelve sons composd
The wondrous building & three Central Domes after the Names
Of his three daughters were encompassd by the twelve bright halls
Every hall surrounded by bright Paradises of Delight
In which are towns & Cities Nations Seas Mountains & Rivers
Each Dome opend toward four halls & the Three Domes Encompassd
The Golden Hall of Urizen whose western side glowd bright
With ever streaming fires beaming from his awful limbs.

VI

The Bands of Heaven flew thro the air singing & shouting to Urizen
Some fix'd the anvil, some the loom erected, some the plow
And harrow formd & framd the harness of silver & ivory
The golden compasses, the quadrant & the rule & balance
They erected the furnaces, they formd the anvils of gold beaten in mills
Where winter beats incessant, fixing them firm on their base
The bellows began to blow & the Lions of Urizen stood round the
anvil
And the leopards coverd with skins of beasts tended the roaring fires
Sublime distinct their lineaments divine of human beauty
The tygers of wrath called the horses of instruction from their mangers
They unloos'd them & put on the harness of gold & silver & ivory
In human forms distinct they stood round Urizen prince of Light
Petrifying all the Human Imagination into rock & sand
Groans ran along Tyburns brook and along the River of Oxford
Among the Druid Temples. Albion groand on Tyburns brook
Albion gave his loud death groan The Atlantic Mountains trembled
Aloft the Moon fled with a cry the Sun with streams of blood
From Albions Loins fled all Peoples and Nations of the Earth
Fled with the noise of Slaughter & the stars of heaven Fled
Jerusalem came down in a dire ruin over all the Earth
She fell cold from Lambeths Vales in groans & Dewy death
The dew of anxious souls the death-sweat of the dying
In every pillard hall & arched roof of Albions skies
The brother & the brother bathe in blood upon the Severn
The Maiden weeping by. The father & the mother with

The Maidens father & her mother fainting over the body
And the Young Man the Murderer fleeing over the mountains.

VII

The ever pitying one who seeth all things saw his fall
And in the dark vacuity created a bosom of clay
When wearied dead he fell his limbs reposd in the bosom of slime
As the seed falls from the sowers hand so Urizen fell & death
Shut up his powers in oblivion. then as the seed shoots forth
In pain & sorrow. So the slimy bed his limbs renewd
At first an infant weakness. periods passd he gatherd strength
But still in solitude he sat then rising threw his flight
Onward tho falling thro the waste of night & ending in death
And in another resurrection to sorrow & weary travel
But still his books he bore in his strong hands & his iron pen
For when he died they lay beside his grave & when he rose
He siezd them with a gloomy smile for wrapd in his death clothes
He hid them when he slept in death when he revivd the clothes
Were rotted by the winds the books remaind still unconsumd
Still to be written & interleavd with brass & iron & gold
Time after time for such a journey none but iron pens
Can write And adamantine leaves recieve nor can the man who goes
The journey obstinate refuse to write time after time
Endless had been his travel but the Divine hand him led
For infinite the distance & obscurd by Combustions dire
By rocky masses frowning in the abysses revolving erratic
Round Lakes of fire in the dark deep the ruins of Urizens world
Oft would he sit in a dark rift & regulate his books
Or sleep such sleep as spirits eternal wearied in his dark
Tearful & sorrowful state. then rise look out & ponder
His dismal voyage eyeing the next sphere tho far remote
Then darting into the Abyss of night his venturous limbs
Thro lightnings thunders earthquakes & concussions fires & floods
Stemming his downward fall labouring up against futurity
Creating many a Vortex fixing many a Science in the deep
And thence throwing his venturous limbs into the Vast unknown
Swift Swift from Chaos to chaos from void to void a road immense
For when he came to where a Vortex ceasd to operate
Nor down nor up remaind then if he turnd & lookd back
From whence he came twas upward all. & if he turnd and viewd
The unpassd void upward was still his mighty wandring

The midst between an Equilibrium grey of air serene
Where he might live in peace & where his life might meet repose.

But Urizen said Can I not leave this world of Cumbrous wheels
Circle oer Circle nor on high attain a void
Where self sustaining I may view all things beneath my feet
Or sinking thro these Elemental wonders swift to fall
I thought perhaps to find an End a world beneath of voidness
Whence I might travel round the outside of this Dark confusion
When I bend downward bending my head downward into the deep
Tis upward all which way soever I my course begin
But when A Vortex formd on high by labour & sorrow & care
And weariness begins on all my limbs then sleep revives
My wearied spirits waking then tis downward all which way
So ever I my spirits turn no end I find of all
O what a world is here unlike those climes of bliss
Where my sons gatherd round my knees O thou poor ruind world
Thou horrible ruin once like me thou wast all glorious
And now like me partaking desolate thy masters lot
Art thou O ruin the once glorious heaven are these thy rocks
Where joy sang in the trees & pleasure sported on the rivers
And laughter sat beneath the Oaks & innocence sported round
Upon the green plains & sweet friendship met in palaces
And books & instruments of song & pictures of delight
Where are they whelmd beneath these ruins in horrible destruction
And if Eternal falling I repose on the dark bosom
Of winds & waters or thence fall into a Void where air
Is not down falling thro immensity ever & ever
I lose my powers weakend every revolution till a death
Shuts up my powers then a seed in the vast womb of darkness
I dwell in dim oblivion. brooding over me the Enormous worlds
Reorganize me shooting forth in bones & flesh & blood
I am regenerated to fall or rise at will or to remain
A labourer of ages a dire discontent a living woe
Wandring in vain.

VIII

Then All in Great Eternity Met in the Council of God
As one Man Even Jesus upon Gilead & Hermon
Upon the Limit of Contraction to create the fallen Man
The Fallen Man stretchd like a Corse upon the oozy Rock
Washd with the tides Pale overgrown with weeds

That movd with horrible dreams hovring high over his head
Two winged immortal shapes one standing at his feet
Toward the East one standing at his head toward the west
Their wings joind in the Zenith over head
Such is a Vision of All Beulah hovring over the Sleeper

The limit of Contraction now was fixd & Man began
To wake upon the Couch of Death he sneezed seven times
A tear of blood dropped from either eye again he reposd
In the saviours arms, in the arms of tender mercy & loving kindness
Then Los said I behold the Divine Vision thro the broken Gates
Of thy poor broken heart astonished melted into Compassion & Love
And Enitharmon said I see the Lamb of God upon Mount Zion
Wondring with love & Awe they felt the divine hand upon them.

IX

The Lamb of God has rent the Veil of Mystery soon to return
In Clouds & Fires around the rock & the Mysterious tree
As the seed waits Eagerly watching for its flower & fruit
Anxious its little soul looks out into the clear expanse
To see if hungry winds are abroad with their invisible army
So Man looks out in tree & herb & fish & bird & beast
Collecting up the scatterd portions of his immortal body
Into the Elemental forms of every thing that grows
He tries the sullen north wind riding on its angry furrows
The sultry south when the sun rises & the angry east
When the sun sets when the clods harden & the cattle stand
Drooping & the birds hide in their silent nests. he stores his thoughts
As in a store house in his memory he regulates the forms
Of all beneath & all above & in the gentle West
Reposes where the Suns heat dwells he rises to the Sun
And to the Planets of the Night & to the stars that gild
The Zodiac & the stars that sullen stand to north & south
He touches the remotest pole & in the Center weeps
That Man should Labour & sorrow & learn & forget & return
To the dark valley whence he came to begin his labours anew
In pain he sighs in pain he labours in his universe
Screaming in birds over the deep & howling in the Wolf
Over the slain & moaning in the cattle & in the winds
And weeping over Orc & Urizen in clouds & flaming fires
And in the cries of birth & in the groans of death his voice
Is heard throughout the Universe wherever a grass grows

Or a leaf buds The Eternal Man is seen is heard is felt
And all his Sorrows till he reassumes his ancient bliss.

X

With thunderous noise & dreadful shakings rocking to & fro
The heavens are shaken & the Earth removed from its place
The foundations of the Eternal hills discoverd
The thrones of Kings are shaken they have lost their robes & crowns
The poor smite their opressors they awake up to the harvest
The naked warriors rush together down to the sea shore
Trembling before the multitudes of slaves now set at liberty
They are become like wintry flocks like forests stripd of leaves
The opressed pursue like the wind there is no room for escape
The Spectre of Enitharmon let loose on the troubled deep
Waild shrill in the confusion.

XI

And all the while the trumpet sounds from the clotted gore & from the
hollow den
Start forth the trembling millions into flames of mental fire
Bathing their limbs in the bright visions of Eternity
Then like the doves from pillars of Smoke the trembling families
Of women & children throughout every nation under heaven
Cling round the men in bands of twenties & of fifties pale
As snow that falls around a leafless tree upon the green
Their opressors are falln they have Stricken them they awake to life

Yet pale the just man stands erect & looking up to heavn
Trembling & strucken by the Universal stroke the trees unroot
The rocks groan horrible & run about. The mountains &
Their rivers cry with a dismal cry the cattle gather together
Lowing they kneel before the heavens. the wild beasts of the forests
Tremble the Lion shuddering asks the Leopard. Feelest thou
The dread I feel unknown before My voice refuses to roar
And in weak moans I speak to thee This night
Before the mornings dawn the Eagle calld the Vulture
The Raven calld the hawk I heard them from my forests black
Saying Let us go up far for soon I smell upon the wind
A terror coming from the South. The Eagle & Hawk fled away
At dawn & Eer the sun arose the raven & Vulture followd

Let us flee also to the north. They fled. The Sons of Men
Saw them depart in dismal droves. The trumpet sounded loud
And all the Sons of Eternity Descended into Beulah.

XII

There is from Great Eternity a mild & pleasant rest
Namd Beulah a Soft Moony Universe feminine lovely
Pure mild & Gentle given in Mercy to those who sleep
Eternally. Created by the Lamb of God around
On all sides within & without the Universal Man
The Daughters of Beulah follow sleepers in all their Dreams
Creating Spaces lest they fall into Eternal Death
The Circle of Destiny complete they gave to it a Space
And namd the Space Ulro & brooded over it in care & love.

XIII

Lo how the Pomp of Mystery goes down into the Caves
Her great men howl & throw the dust & rend their hoary hair
Her delicate women & children shriek upon the bitter wind
Spoild of their beauty their hair rent & their skin shriveled up
Lo darkness covers the long pomp of banners on the wind
And black horses & armed men & miserable bound captives
Where shall the graves recieve them all & where shall be their place
And who shall mourn for Mystery who never loosd her Captives
Let the slave grinding at the mill run out into the field
Let him look up into the heavens & laugh in the bright air
Let the inchaind soul shut up in darkness & in sighing
Whose face has never seen a smile in thirty weary years
Rise & look out his chains are loose his dungeon doors are open
And let his wife & children return from the opressors scourge
They look behind at every step & believe it is a dream
Are these the Slaves that groand along the streets of Mystery
Where are your bonds & task masters are these the prisoners
Where are your chains where are your tears why do you look around
If you are thirsty there is the river go bathe your parched limbs
The good of all the Land is before you for Mystery is no more.

Songs of joy from *The Four Zoas*

I

Come forth O Vala from the grass & from the silent Dew
Rise from the dews of death for the Eternal Man is Risen
She rises among flowers & looks toward the Eastern clearness
She walks yea runs her feet are wingd on the tops of the bending grass
Her garments rejoice in the vocal wind & her hair glistens with dew
She answerd thus Whose voice is this in the voice of the nourishing air
In the spirit of the morning awaking the Soul from its grassy bed
Where dost thou dwell for it is thee I seek & but for thee
I must have slept Eternally nor have felt the dew of thy morning
Look how the opening dawn advances with vocal harmony
Look how the beams foreshew the rising of some glorious power
The sun is thine he goeth forth in his majestic brightness
O thou creating voice that callest & who shall answer thee

Where dost thou flee O fair one where dost thou seek thy happy place

To yonder brightness there I haste for sure I came from thence
Or I must have slept eternally nor have felt the dew of morning

Eternally thou must have slept nor have felt the morning dew
But for yon nourishing sun tis that by which thou art arisen
The birds adore the sun the beasts rise up & play in his beams
And every flower & every leaf rejoices in his light
Then O thou fair one sit thee down for thou art as the grass
Thou risest in the dew of morning & at night art folded up

Alas am I but as a flower then will I sit me down
Then will I weep then Ill complain & sigh for immortality
And chide my maker thee O Sun that raisedst me to fall

So saying she sat down & wept beneath the apple trees
O be thou blotted out thou Sun that raisedst me to trouble
That gavest me a heart to crave & raisedst me thy phantom
To feel thy heat & see thy light & wander here alone
Hopeless if I am like the grass & so shall pass away

Rise sluggish Soul why sitst thou here why dost thou sit & weep
Yon Sun shall wax old & decay but thou shalt ever flourish

The fruit shall ripen & fall down & the flowers consume away
But thou shalt still survive arise O dry thy dewy tears

Hah! Shall I still survive whence came that sweet & comforting voice
And whence that voice of sorrow O sun thou art nothing now to me
Go on thy course rejoicing & let us both rejoice together
I walk among his flocks & hear the bleating of his lambs
O that I could behold his face & follow his pure feet
I walk by the footsteps of his flocks come hither tender flocks
Can you converse with a pure Soul that seeketh for her maker
You answer not then am I set your mistress in this garden
Ill watch you & attend your footsteps you are not like the birds
That sing & fly in the bright air but you do lick my feet
And let me touch your wooly backs follow me as I sing
For in my bosom a new song arises to my Lord
Rise up O Sun most glorious minister & light of day
Flow on ye gentle airs & bear the voice of my rejoicing
Wave freshly clear waters flowing around the tender grass
And thou sweet smelling ground put forth thy life in fruits & flowers
Follow me O my flocks & hear me sing my rapturous Song
I will cause my voice to be heard on the clouds that glitter in the sun
I will call & who shall answer me I will sing who shall reply
For from my pleasant hills behold the living living springs
Running among my green pastures delighting among my trees
I am not here alone my flocks you are my brethren
And you birds that sing & adorn the sky you are my sisters
I sing & you reply to my Song I rejoice & you are glad
Follow me O my flocks we will now descend into the valley
O how delicious are the grapes flourishing in the Sun
How clear the spring of the rock running among the golden sand
How cool the breezes of the vally & the arms of the branchy trees
Cover us from the Sun come & let us sit in the Shade
My Luvah here hath placd me in a Sweet & pleasant Land
And given me fruits & pleasant waters & warm hills & cool valleys
Here will I build myself a house & here Ill call on his name
Here Ill return when I am weary & take my pleasant rest.

II

The falling Grapes that odorous burst upon the winds. Arise
My flocks & herds trample the Corn my cattle browze upon
The ripe Clusters The shepherds shout for Luvah prince of Love
Let the Bulls of Luvah tread the Corn & draw the loaded waggon

Into the Barn while children glean the Ears around the door
Then shall they lift their innocent hands & stroke his furious nose
And he shall lick the little girls white neck & on her head
Scatter the perfume of his breath while from his mountains high
The lion of terror shall come down & bending his bright mane
And couching at their side shall eat from the curld boys white lap
His golden food and in the evening sleep before the Door.
Attempting to be more than Man We become less said Luvah
As he arose from the bright feast drunk with the wine of ages.

III

Timbrels & Violins sport round the Wine Presses The little Seed
The Sportive root the Earthworm the small beetle the wise Emmet
Dance round the Wine Presses of Luvah. the Centipede is there
The ground Spider with many Eyes the Mole clothed in Velvet
The Earwig armd the tender maggot emblem of Immortality
The Slow Slug the grasshopper that sings & laughs & drinks
The winter comes he folds his slender bones without a murmur
There is the Nettle that stings with soft down & there
The indignant Thistle whose bitterness is bred in his milk
And who lives on the contempt of his neighbour there all the idle
    weeds
That creep about the obscure places shew their various limbs
Naked in all their beauty dancing round the Wine Presses.

IV

The Sun has left his blackness & has found a fresher morning
And the mild moon rejoices in the clear & cloudless night
And Man walks forth from midst of the fires the evil is all consumd
His eyes behold the Angelic spheres arising night & day
The stars consumd like a lamp blown out & in their stead behold
The Expanding Eyes of Man behold the depths of wondrous worlds
One Earth one sea beneath nor Erring Globes wander but Stars
Of fire rise up nightly from the Ocean & one Sun
Each morning like a New born Man issues with songs & Joy
Calling the Plowman to his Labour & the Shepherd to his rest
He walks upon the Eternal Mountains raising his heavenly voice.
Conversing with the Animal forms of wisdom night & day
That risen from the Sea of fire renewd walk oer the Earth.

Poems from Blake's Notebook

I

Mock on Mock on Voltaire Rousseau
Mock on Mock on! tis all in vain!
You throw the sand against the wind
And the wind blows it back again

And every sand becomes a Gem
Reflected in the beams divine
Blown back they blind the mocking Eye
But still in Israels paths they shine

The Atoms of Democritus
And Newtons Particles of light
Are sands upon the Red sea shore
Where Israels tents do shine so bright

II

To my Mirtle

To a lovely mirtle bound
Blossoms showring all around
O how sick & weary I
Underneath my mirtle lie
Why should I be bound to thee
O my lovely mirtle tree

III

I feard the fury of my wind
Would blight all blossoms fair & true
And my sun it shind & shind
And my wind it never blew

But a blossom fair or true
Was not found on any tree
For all blossoms grew & grew
Fruitless false tho fair to see

IV

I saw a chapel all of gold
That none did dare to enter in
And many weeping stood without
Weeping mourning worshipping

I saw a serpent rise between
The white pillars of the door
And he forcd & forcd & forcd
Down the golden hinges tore

And along the pavement sweet
Set with pearls & rubies bright
All his slimy length he drew
Till upon the altar white

Vomiting his poison out
On the bread & on the wine
So I turnd into a sty
And laid me down among the swine

V

I laid me down upon a bank
Where love lay sleeping
I heard among the rushes dank
Weeping Weeping

Then I went to the heath & the wild
To the thistles & thorns of the waste
And they told me how they were beguild
Driven out & compeld to be chaste

VI

To Nobodaddy

Why art thou silent & invisible
Father of Jealousy
Why dost thou hide thyself in clouds
From every searching Eye

Why darkness & obscurity
In all thy words & laws
That none dare eat the fruit but from
The wily serpents jaws
Or is it because Secresy
Gains females loud applause

VII

Are not the joys of morning sweeter
Than the joys of night
And are the vigorous joys of youth
Ashamed of the light

Let age & sickness silent rob
The vineyards in the night
But those who burn with vigrous youth
Pluck fruits before the light

Poems in manuscript

I

The Land of Dreams

Awake awake my little Boy
Thou wast thy Mothers only joy
Why dost thou weep in thy gentle sleep
Awake thy Father does thee keep

O what Land is the Land of Dreams
What are its Mountains & what are its Streams
O Father I saw my Mother there
Among the Lillies by waters fair

Among the Lambs clothed in white
She walkd with her Thomas in sweet delight
I wept for joy like a dove I mourn
O when shall I again return

Dear Child I also by pleasant Streams
Have wanderd all Night in the Land of Dreams
But tho calm & warm the Waters wide
I could not get to the other side

Father O Father what do we here
In this Land of unbelief & fear
The Land of Dreams is better far
Above the light of the Morning Star

II

Mary

Sweet Mary the first time she ever was there
Came into the Ball room among the Fair
The young Men & Maidens around her throng
And these are the words upon every tongue

An Angel is here from the heavenly Climes
Or again does return the Golden times

Her eyes outshine every brilliant ray
She opens her lips tis the Month of May

Mary moves in soft beauty & conscious delight
To augment with sweet smiles all the joys of the Night
Nor once blushes to own to the rest of the Fair
That sweet Love & Beauty are worthy our care

In the Morning the Villagers rose with delight
And repeated with pleasure the joys of the night
And Mary arose among Friends to be free
But no Friend from henceforward thou Mary shalt see

Some said she was proud some calld her a whore
And some when she passed by shut to the door
A damp cold came oer her her blushes all fled
Her lillies & roses are blighted & shed

O why was I born with a different Face
Why was I not born like this Envious Race
Why did Heaven adorn me with bountiful hand
And then set me down in an envious Land

To be weak as a Lamb & smooth as a Dove
And not to raise Envy is calld Christian Love
But if you raise Envy your Merits to blame
For planting such spite in the weak & the tame

I will humble my Beauty I will not dress fine
I will keep from the Ball & my Eyes shall not shine
And if any Girls Lover forsakes her for me
I'll refuse him my hand & from Envy be free

She went out in Morning attird plain & neat
Proud Marys gone Mad said the Child in the Street
She went out in Morning in plain neat attire
And came home in Evening bespatterd with mire

She trembled & wept sitting on the Bed side
She forgot it was Night & she trembled & cried
She forgot it was Night she forgot it was Morn
Her soft Memory imprinted with Faces of Scorn

With Faces of Scorn & with Eyes of disdain
Like foul Fiends inhabiting Marys mild Brain

She remembers no Face like the Human Divine
All Faces have Envy sweet Mary but thine

And thine is a Face of sweet Love in Despair
And thine is a Face of mild sorrow & care
And thine is a Face of wild terror & fear
That shall never be quiet till laid on its bier

III

Long John Brown & Little Mary Bell

Little Mary Bell had a Fairy in a Nut
Long John Brown had the Devil in his Gut
Long John Brown lovd Little Mary Bell
And the Fairy drew the Devil into the Nut-shell

Her Fairy skipd out & her Fairy skipd in
He laughd at the Devil saying Love is a Sin
The Devil he raged & the Devil he was wroth
And the Devil enterd into the Young Mans broth

He was soon in the Gut of the loving Young Swain
For John eat & drank to drive away Loves pain
But all he could do he grew thinner & thinner
Tho he eat & drank as much as ten Men for his dinner

Some said he had a Wolf in his stomach day & night
Some said he had the Devil & they guessd right
The fairy skipd about in his Glory Joy & Pride
And he laughd at the Devil till poor John Brown died

Then the Fairy skipd out of the old Nut shell
And woe & alack for Pretty Mary Bell
For the Devil crept in when The Fairy skipd out
And there goes Miss Bell with her fusty old Nut

Auguries of Innocence

To see a World in a Grain of Sand
And a Heaven in a Wild Flower
Hold Infinity in the palm of your hand
And Eternity in an hour
He who mocks the Infants Faith
Shall be mock'd in Age & Death
He who shall teach the Child to Doubt
The rotting Grave shall neer get out
He who respects the Infants faith
Triumphs over Hell & Death
The Childs Toys & the Old Mans Reasons
Are the Fruits of the Two seasons
The Questioner who sits so sly
Shall never know how to Reply
He who replies to words of Doubt
Doth put the Light of Knowledge out
The Strongest Poison ever known
Came from Caesars Laurel Crown
Nought can Deform the Human Race
Like to the Armours iron brace
When Gold & Gems adorn the Plow
To peaceful Arts shall Envy Bow
A Riddle or the Crickets Cry
Is to Doubt a fit Reply
The Emmets Inch & Eagles Mile
Make Lame Philosophy to smile
He who Doubts from what he sees
Will neer Believe do what you Please
If the Sun & Moon should Doubt
Theyd immediately Go out
A Robin Red breast in a Cage
Puts all Heaven in a Rage
A Dove house filld with Doves & Pigeons
Shudders Hell thro all its regions
A dog starvd at his Masters Gate
Predicts the ruin of the State
A Horse misusd upon the Road

Calls to Heaven for Human blood
Each outcry of the hunted Hare
A fibre from the Brain does tear
A Skylark wounded in the wing
A Cherubim does cease to sing
The Game Cock clipd & armd for fight
Does the Rising Sun affright
Every Wolfs & Lions howl
Raises from Hell a Human Soul
The wild deer wandring here & there
Keeps the Human Soul from Care
The Lamb misusd breeds Public Strife
And yet forgives the Butchers Knife
The Bat that flits at close of Eve
Has left the Brain that wont Believe
The Owl that calls upon the Night
Speaks the Unbelievers fright
He who shall hurt the little Wren
Shall never be belovd by Men
He who the Ox to wrath has movd
Shall never be by Woman lovd
The wanton Boy that kills the Fly
Shall feel the Spiders enmity
He who torments the Chafers sprite
Weaves a Bower in endless Night
The Catterpiller on the Leaf
Repeats to thee thy Mothers grief
Kill not the Moth nor Butterfly
For the Last Judgment draweth nigh
He who shall train the Horse to War
Shall never pass the Polar Bar
The Beggers Dog & Widows Cat
Feed them & thou wilt grow fat
The Gnat that sings his Summers song
Poison gets from Slanders tongue
The poison of the Snake & Newt
Is the sweat of Envys Foot
The Poison of the Honey Bee
Is the Artists Jealousy
The Princes Robes & Beggars Rags
Are Toadstools on the Misers Bags
A Truth thats told with bad intent

Beats all the Lies you can invent
It is right it should be so
Man was made for Joy & Woe
And when this we rightly know
Thro the World we safely go
Joy & Woe are woven fine
A Clothing for the soul divine
Under every grief & pine
Runs a joy with silken twine
The Babe is more than swadling Bands
Throughout all these Human Lands
Tools were made & Born were hands
Every Farmer Understands
Every Tear from Every Eye
Becomes a Babe in Eternity
This is caught by Females bright
And returnd to its own delight
The Bleat the Bark Bellow & Roar
Are Waves that Beat on Heavens Shore
The Babe that weeps the Rod beneath
Writes Revenge in realms of Death
The Beggars Rags fluttering in Air
Does to Rags the Heavens tear
The Soldier armd with Sword & Gun
Palsied strikes the Summers Sun
The poor Mans Farthing is worth more
Than all the Gold on Africs Shore
One Mite wrung from the Labrers hands
Shall buy & sell the Misers Lands
Or if protected from on high
Does that whole Nation sell & buy
To be in a Passion you Good may Do
But no Good if a Passion is in you
The Whore & Gambler by the State
Licencd build that Nations Fate
The Harlots cry from Street to Street
Shall weave Old Englands winding Sheet
The Winners Shout the Losers Curse
Dance before dead Englands Hearse
Every Night & every Morn
Some to Misery are Born
Every Morn & every Night

Some are Born to sweet delight
Some are Born to sweet delight
Some are Born to Endless Night
We are led to Believe a Lie
When we see not Thro the Eye
Which was Born in a Night to perish in a Night
When the Soul Slept in Beams of Light
God Appears & God is Light
To those poor Souls who dwell in Night
But does a Human Form Display
To those who Dwell in Realms of day